PRAISE FOR L

"LEADERSHIP UNDER FIRE: LESSONS FROM THE FRONT LINES OF LAW ENFORCEMENT is a powerful and inspiring guide to real-world leadership. Keith Grounsell masterfully blends personal experience with timeless leadership principles that resonate across both law enforcement and the private sector. His honesty, vulnerability, and commitment to growth make this a must-read for anyone seeking to lead with integrity and courage. This book will not only challenge you but inspire you to be the best leader you can be. A truly superb and transformative work!" - Carl David: Fine Art Dealer / Author / Suicide Prevention Advocate / Law Enforcement Force Multiplier

"LEADERSHIP UNDER FIRE is an engaging and thought-provoking book that delves into the complexities of leadership during times of intense pressure. The author's ability to blend personal stories with actionable leadership strategies sets this book apart. It's not just a collection of theories—it's a practical roadmap for leaders who want to make tough decisions while maintaining their moral compass. The insights on integrity, resilience, and accountability are invaluable for anyone aspiring to lead effectively in challenging environments. A compelling read for leaders at any stage of their journey." - Beta Reader LGT

"Keith exemplifies great leadership in every sense. He is a man whose integrity has never tarnished his badge, serving as a true inspiration to all of us. His unwavering commitment to excellence in his craft he always wants to do better and his ability to develop those around him have profoundly shaped my own journey as a leader. He is a cops cop and I have watched over the last 12 years him develop into a staple in police leadership. Thanks to Keith, I am now sought out to support departmental development and enhance the skills of officers, just as he once did for me. He has finally sat down and wrote a book that gives future leaders the talks and skills and knowledge he instilled in me.

LEADERSHIP UNDER FIRE takes you behind the scenes with us, behind the closed doors, having been a part of his struggles and what kept him up at night. In this book Keith gives you knowledge to overcome obstacles and navigate the world of municipal policing and the landmines of municipal government. The book takes you on the journey of his growth in leading with empathy, transparency, and fairness, and his aim to build strong relationships based on mutual understanding and collaboration with his team. His impact is immeasurable, and his legacy of nurturing future leaders like me will continue to resonate for years to come."- Brandon Davis: Lieutenant Municipal PD in SC / Medic / Instructor / Aspiring Chief of Police.

"LEADERSHIP UNDER FIRE is a powerful and insightful exploration of what it truly means to lead with integrity in the face of adversity. The author draws from deep personal experience, providing real-world examples of leadership in some of the most challenging environments imaginable. From law enforcement to public service, the lessons shared are not only practical but inspiring. This book is a must-read for anyone looking to understand the essence of courageous, principled leadership and how to navigate tough decisions while staying true to one's values. It's both a guide and a testament to the power of leading with honor."- Beta Reader LKS

"This is a gripping and authoritative guide on leadership that combines real-world experience with invaluable lessons on integrity and resilience." - Major Literary Agency based in NYC

"Packed with real-world wisdom and battle-tested strategies, LEADERSHIP UNDER FIRE is a must-read for anyone in leadership or crisis management. Keith Grounsell's experience in high-stakes environments shines through as he shares invaluable lessons on integrity, perseverance, and leading with courage when it matters most. Whether you're in law enforcement, business, or any position of authority, this book will leave you inspired to lead with conviction and face adversity head-on. A true leadership guide from someone who's walked the walk." - Retired 30-Year Law Enforcement Leader

"LEADERSHIP UNDER FIRE is a masterclass in leading with integrity and courage under the toughest conditions." - Beta Reader JS

"LEADERSHIP UNDER FIRE is an exceptional work that brilliantly captures the essence of true leadership. Keith Grounsell's experiences in both law enforcement and the private sector reveal his versatility and profound understanding of what it means to inspire and lead others. His willingness to share his knowledge and personal experiences speaks volumes about his integrity and commitment to uplifting future leaders. Having known and worked with Keith for over 25 years, I can personally attest to his dedication, wisdom, and impact. This book is not just a guide—it's a testament to the lasting influence of great leaders." - Margaret Ruse: 39-Year Veteran Public Servant in Police, Fire, EMS & 911

"LEADERSHIP UNDER FIRE: LESSONS FROM THE FRONT LINES OF LAW ENFORCEMENT is an incredible book for any leader looking to hone, improve, or learn excellent leadership skills. Keith's unparalleled leadership experience in various organizations spanning several continents has given him real-world leadership experience and lessons he passes on to the reader. Keith did a great job of intertwining stories into his leadership lessons, which makes the book even more impactful. The book should have a stamp that says "Battle Tested" on the cover because the leadership lessons Keith espouses have been tested on the front lines of high-stakes leadership. Keith doesn't just talk the talk. He has walked the walk.

Keith is one of the most incredible leaders I have ever met. From the moment we met at an FBI law enforcement executive training session, I knew he was different. He is one of the most motivated and driven leaders you will ever encounter, and his mind is brilliant. Anyone who meets Keith or reads one of his books will walk away from the experience as a better person and leader." - Adam R. Salyards: Chief of Police | Leadership Coach | Organizational Consultant

LEADERSHIP UNDER FIRE

LESSONS FROM THE FRONT LINES OF LAW ENFORCEMENT

KEITH GROUNSELL

CONTENTS

Praise for Leadership Under Fire i
Legal Disclaimer xv
Introduction 1
    The Foundation of Leadership 1
    The Journey of Growth and Service 1

Chapter 1: Leading with Integrity 3
    Doing the Right Thing Even When Your Supervisor Disagrees 4
    Integrity: The Cornerstone of Leadership in Any Organization 5
    Consistency Brings Stability 6
    A Long-Term View of Success 6
    Leading with Integrity at Every Level 7
    Conclusion: Integrity as the Core of Leadership 9

Chapter 2: Discovering Your Leadership Identity 11
    Dynamic Leader: Driving Change and Inspiring Bold Decisions 11
    Hands-On Leader: Leading by Example and Staying Engaged 13
    Servant Leader: Prioritizing People, Building Trust, and Righting Wrongs 14
    Strategic Leader: Thinking Long-Term and Making Informed Decisions 16
    Collaborative Leader: Fostering Teamwork and Inclusivity 17
    Authoritative Leader: Fostering Teamwork and Inclusivity 17
    Innovative Leader: Embracing Change and Encouraging Creativity 19
    Adaptive Leader: Flexibility in the Face of Change 20

    Blending Leadership Styles for Success 21
    Getting to Know Yourself as a Leader 21
Chapter 3: Proactive Leadership: A Path to Success 23
    The Link Between Procrastination and Reactive Leadership 24
    The History of Reactive Policing 25
    A Case for Proactive Police Work 27
    The Role of Servant Leadership in Proactive Leadership 28
    Conclusion: Proactive Leadership is Key to Success 29
Chapter 4: Crisis Management 33
    Leadership in Liberia During the COVID-19 Pandemic 34
    Lessons for Crisis Management in the Business World 35
    Crisis Management in Law Enforcement and Beyond 37
    Conclusion: Leadership in Crisis 39
Chapter 5: Building and Leading Effective Teams 41
    Trust as the Foundation 42
    Communication as a Critical Component 42
    Accountability as a Pillar 43
    Empowering Your Team 44
    The Power of Motivation in Leadership 45
    The Employee Action Committee: Giving the Team a Voice 46
    Building Trust Through Vulnerability 48
    Leading With Purpose 48
Chapter 6: Community-Centered Leadership 51
    Engaging Directly with the Community 52
    Cancer Awareness Initiative 53
    Transparency and Building Trust 54
    Tailoring Leadership to Diverse Communities 55
    The Power of Reciprocity in Community-Centered Leadership 55

Leadership as a Service 56

Conclusion: A Universal Approach to Leadership 56

Chapter 7: The Ability to Make Decisions 59

I. The Importance of Decisiveness 59

II. Owning Mistakes and Driving Change 60

III. Impact of Leadership on Organizational Culture 61

IV. Handling Opposition 62

V. Decision-Making in Leadership: A Common Principle in Law Enforcement and Business 63

Conclusion 63

Chapter 8: Progressive Discipline and Accountability 65

Progressive Discipline: A Fair Approach 65

The Fine Line Between Correction and Morale 66

The Challenges of Accountability 67

FDD Story: Accountability on a Larger Scale 67

Chapter 9: Termination, Layoffs, and Empathetic Leadership ... 69

Termination: Balancing Tough Decisions with Humanity 69

Layoffs: Compassion in the Face of Business Decisions 70

Corporate Parallels: Empathy and Dignity in the Boardroom 71

Chapter 10: Why People Don't Quit Jobs, They Quit Leaders 73

The Importance of Diverse Leadership Backgrounds 73

Retention and Leadership Turnover 75

Creating a Culture That Retains Talent 77

The Ability to Make Decisions 78

Finding the Right Fit 79

The Role of Leadership in Retention, with a Focus on Officer Wellness 79

Supporting Employee Well-Being through Leadership 80

Conclusion 80

Chapter 11: The Art of Delegation and Empowerment 83
The Struggle with Letting Go 83

The Pitfalls of Micromanagement and the Power of Trust 84

Empowering the Team 85

Putting Your Best Foot Forward in Leadership 86

Avoiding the Pitfall of Overworking Your Best People 88

The Importance of Rewarding and Promoting Talent 89

The Benefits of Delegation 90

How to Delegate Effectively 91

The Impact of Delegation on Leadership 91

Chapter 12: Adapting to Cultural Challenges 93
Adapting Leadership Style in Diverse Communities 96

Cultural Adaptability in Crisis Situations 97

The Importance of Recruiting a Diverse Workforce 98

Adapting Leadership to Cultural Challenges in the Private Sector
.... 100

Conclusion 101

Chapter 13: Leadership and Technology 103
Data-Driven Decision Making: Allocating Resources Effectively 104

AI: The Present and Future of Leadership 104

License Plate Readers: A Force Multiplier for Law Enforcement 106

Office of Investigative Technology: Leveraging Digital Evidence
.... 106

Integrating Technology into Daily Operations 108

The Ethical Use of Technology 108

The Human Element: Technology and Empathy 109

Conclusion: Balancing Technology with Human Leadership 110

ix

Chapter 14: Ethics and Leadership 111
    Ethical Challenges Faced During My Time as Chief of Police 111
    Keen Sense of Justice in Leadership 114
    Ethics Extend Beyond Being Chief of Police 115
    Personal Ethics and Professional Integrity 116
    Conclusion: Ethical Leadership as a Legacy 117

Chapter 15: Navigating Organizational Politics 119
    Appearing Neutral and Serving Everyone 119
    Neutrality in Leadership 121
    Knowing the Hills You're Willing to Die On 122
    Balancing Political Needs with Integrity 123
    Transparency: A Double-Edged Sword 123
    Fairness and Perception 126
    Navigating the Political Landscape 127
    The Importance of Strategic Communication 128
    Beware of Misunderstandings in Digital Communication 129
    Context Matters in Strategic Communication 130
    Strategic Communication in Crisis Situations 131
    Mastering the Art of Communication 132
    Conclusion: Leadership Beyond Politics 132

Chapter 16: Encouraging Positive Culture Through Celebrating Successes 135
    The Power of Recognition 135
    Celebrating Successes Without Overdoing It 136
    Transforming the Personnel File 136
    Building Loyalty Through Caring Leadership 137
    Fostering a Culture of Excellence 138
    The Power of Pushing Beyond Comfort Zones 138

    Creating a Lasting Impact 139

    Encouraging Growth While Maintaining Balance 140

Chapter 17: Facing Adversity in Leadership 141

    Introduction: Resilience and Growth Through Adversity 141

    Standing on Integrity: Ethical Leadership in the Face of Challenges
    141

    Resilience in the Face of Challenges: The Role of Support Systems
    and Personal Strength 142

    Navigating Public Criticism with Resilience and Integrity:
    Leadership Under Public Scrutiny 143

    Operation Good Time: Leadership in the Face of Political Pressure
    143

Chapter 18: Thriving Through Adversity 147

    Dynamic Leadership and Political Realities: Adapting Leadership in
    an Unstable Environment 147

    Navigating Leadership and Relationships: Trust and Loyalty in
    Leadership 148

    The Challenge of Scrutiny and Shortened Tenures: Adapting to
    Modern Leadership Realities 148

    Learning from Setbacks: Turning Adversity into Leadership Growth
    149

    Maintaining a Positive Outlook 149

    Turning Setbacks into Opportunities 150

    Conclusion: Lessons on Resilience from Adversity 150

Chapter 19: Transitioning Leadership Across Industries 153

    Understanding the Parallels Between Law Enforcement and
    Corporate Leadership 154

    Transferable Leadership Skills: From Law Enforcement to
    Corporate America (and Beyond) 154

    Crisis Management: Staying Calm Under Pressure 154

Decision-Making and Accountability: Leading With Integrity 155

Building and Leading Effective Teams in High-Stress Environments 156

Integrity and a Clear Background as Cornerstones of Leadership 157

Outlets Outside of Work: Maintaining Work-Life Balance 158

Compensation and Work-Life Balance: Understanding the Trade-Offs 158

Corporate to Command Staff: Reverse Transitions and Cross-Industry Leadership 159

Conclusion: Leadership Adaptability Across Different Environments 160

Conclusion: The Legacy of Leadership 161
Conclusion: The Legacy of Leadership 162

Bonus Section: Perfecting the Interview to Land the Position You Desire 163
1. Confidence vs. Arrogance 163
2. Turning Negatives into Positives 164
3. Dressing the Part 165
4. Greeting the Panel 165
5. Asking Insightful Questions 166
6. Be Well-Groomed 166
7. Research and Preparation 167
8. Understanding the Role 167
9. Study the Budget and Social Media 167
10. Have Your Answers Ready 168
11. Personalize Yourself 168
12. Show How Much You Care 169
Tying it All Together 169

Bonus Section: The Essential Traits of a Successful Leader 171
    Setting Clear Goals 171

    Consistency 172

    Happiness 172

    Finding Your Purpose 173

    Faith and Spirituality 173

    Love and Compassion 173

    Health and Well-being 174

    Positivity and Optimism 174

    Caring for Others 174

    Conclusion: The Path to Leadership Success 175

150 Leadership Questions and Answers 176
Appendix- Leadership Workbook and Action Plans 191
    Purpose and Intent: 191

Acknowledgments and Tribute 215
About the Author 217
Other Great Reads By This Same Author 219

LEGAL DISCLAIMER

The stories, scenarios, and experiences presented in *Leadership Under Fire: Lessons from the Frontlines of Law Enforcement* are based on the real-life experiences of the author, Keith Grounsell. While every effort has been made to accurately recount these events, certain names, locations, dates, and identifying details have been modified to protect the privacy of individuals and to comply with applicable privacy laws.

This book is intended for educational and informational purposes only. The content is not a substitute for professional advice or training, and the techniques, strategies, and recommendations outlined are not guaranteed to produce any specific outcomes. Readers should use their own judgment and seek legal, professional, or expert advice before implementing any actions or strategies discussed in this book. The author and publisher disclaim any liability for any direct, indirect, or consequential loss, injury, or damage resulting from the use or misuse of the information contained within.

Where critical discussions of actions or behaviors are presented, they are based on the author's recollection of events and are included for the purpose of sharing leadership lessons. These accounts reflect the author's personal perspective and are not intended to defame, malign, or harm the reputation of any individual or entity, living or deceased. Any opinions expressed are those of the author and are presented in good faith, based on the author's understanding of the circumstances at the time. No statement is made or intended as a factual assertion regarding any individual's personal character, unless based on public records or legal findings.

By reading this book, you agree that the author, Keith Grounsell, and the publisher shall not be held liable for any direct, indirect, incidental, or consequential damages or losses arising from the use of, or reliance on, the information provided.

This book is protected by copyright law, and no part of it may be reproduced, distributed, or transmitted in any form or by any means without the prior written permission of the author and publisher, except for brief quotations in a review or scholarly analysis, in compliance with fair use standards.

Copyright © 2024 by KPG Enterprises, LLC.

All rights reserved

INTRODUCTION

The Foundation of Leadership

Leadership is more than just a title or position—it's about influence, responsibility, and the ability to inspire others to achieve a common goal. The foundation of leadership lies in a deep understanding of ethical principles, personal integrity, and the commitment to serve others. Throughout my career, I've learned that strong leadership is built on a foundation of trust, respect, and the relentless pursuit of excellence. This book explores the essential qualities that every leader must cultivate to be effective, including integrity, decisiveness, and the ability to adapt to change.

As you read through these chapters, you'll discover that leadership is not a one-size-fits-all concept. It's a dynamic and evolving practice that requires continuous growth and learning. Whether you're leading a small team or an entire organization, the principles discussed in this book will help you build a solid foundation for your leadership journey.

The Journey of Growth and Service

Leadership is a journey, not a destination. It's about growing, learning, and adapting while serving those you lead. My journey in leadership has been shaped by the challenges I've faced and the people I've had the privilege to work with. From my early days in law enforcement to my roles as Chief of Police in multiple cities, I've learned that true leadership is about service—putting the needs of others above your own and guiding your team towards success.

Throughout this book, you'll find stories and lessons from my own experiences, as well as practical advice on how to navigate the complexities of leadership. Whether it's handling a crisis, building a strong team, or making tough decisions, the insights shared here are designed to help you grow as a leader and better serve those around you.

Leadership is not about being in charge; it's about taking care of those in your charge. It's about making decisions that are in the best interest of your team and the organization, even when those decisions are difficult. It's about being a role model, setting the standard for others to follow, and creating a positive culture where everyone can thrive.

As you embark on your own leadership journey, remember that the path is not always easy, but it is always rewarding. The growth you experience and the impact you have on others will be your greatest achievements. This book is your guide to becoming the leader you were meant to be—a leader who inspires, motivates, and makes a lasting difference.

CHAPTER 1:

LEADING WITH INTEGRITY

Integrity isn't just a trait; it's the foundation upon which all true leadership is built. Throughout my career in law enforcement, from my days as an undercover narcotics officer to my role as Chief of Police in Simpsonville and Laurens, South Carolina, integrity has been my guiding principle. Leadership demands honesty, transparency, and a steadfast commitment to doing what's right—even when it's the hardest path to take.

When I first took on the role of Chief of Police in Simpsonville, the department faced significant challenges. Crime rates were high, community trust was low, and rumors of police corruption were widespread. The agency was severely understaffed, struggling to fill positions, and department morale was at an all-time low. I knew the only way to turn things around was to rebuild trust—both within the department and with the community we served. This required a commitment to integrity that had to start from the top.

One of the first steps I took was to implement dozens of community-based policing programs. These initiatives were designed not just to reduce crime, but to engage the community in the process. We created programs that focused on everything from youth outreach to neighborhood watch groups. The results were remarkable: within two years, Simpsonville went from being ranked the 28th safest city in South Carolina to the number one spot. This wasn't just about enforcing the law; it was about leading with integrity and showing the community that we were there to serve and protect them honestly and transparently.

But leading with integrity isn't just about implementing programs or policies; it's about making tough decisions that may not always be popular. During my tenure in Simpsonville, I faced a situation that tested my commitment to integrity like never before. The mayor at the time was involved in protecting individuals who were covering up ethics violations and crimes committed by city officials, and he expected me to do the same. While the easy path would have been to look the other way, doing so would have betrayed the very principles I had sworn to uphold and lived by. Instead, I pursued a specific cold case relentlessly, which led to the exposure of police corruption that had spanned decades. The lead investigator for the department, who had served before my time as Chief of Police, eventually pled guilty to intentionally destroying evidence to protect white suspects in a racially motivated rape and murder. As a result, the mayor's other wrongdoings came to light, and he was charged and found guilty after a three-day trial of two offenses involving crimes of moral turpitude, rendering him ineligible to hold public office in South Carolina again.

Doing the Right Thing Even When Your Supervisor Disagrees

In my first role as Chief of Police, I faced a situation that tested my commitment to doing the right thing, even when my supervisor didn't agree. Before taking on this leadership position, I had been the Lead Investigator for the Solicitor in the largest prosecutor's office in South Carolina. One key piece of advice the Solicitor gave me before I left was to have the state law enforcement conduct a full audit of the Property & Evidence (P&E) room as one of my first actions. This was crucial to ensure a clean slate regarding the evidentiary items in the department's possession—some of which dated back more than a hundred years.

When I presented this plan to my city administrator, he didn't agree with my decision. He felt it was unnecessary, but I respectfully explained the importance of accountability and knowing exactly what we were responsible for. Despite his objections, I proceeded with the audit. It took almost a full week, with thousands of pages making up the final report.

This decision became particularly significant when allegations surfaced regarding a piece of evidence from a murder and rape case dating back over 20 years. It was discovered that a key piece of evidence—a hair sample signed out for DNA testing seven years earlier—had never reached the state lab. My audit of the P&E room played a pivotal role in uncovering this discrepancy. The investigation revealed that the evidence had been tampered with by the previous head of investigations before my tenure. As a result, the case was tainted, and the court ruled that the evidence could not be used—forever preventing justice for the victim's family.

Had I not conducted this audit, I might have been blamed for the missing evidence, and the integrity of my administration would have been questioned. This situation serves as a critical lesson for new chiefs of police or sheriffs: having a neutral, detached, outside law enforcement agency perform an audit of the P&E room during your first week is not just good practice—it's essential for protecting both your administration and the justice system.

Integrity: The Cornerstone of Leadership in Any Organization

The principles of integrity in leadership are not confined to law enforcement; they span every level of leadership in any organization, whether in government or the private sector. In any leadership role, doing the right thing is rarely the easiest choice, but it's always the most important one. Leaders who consistently act with integrity set the tone for their organization, creating an environment where people know they can trust their decisions.

In corporate America, as in law enforcement, integrity builds stability amidst uncertainty. When leaders consistently make decisions based on principles rather than convenience, they create a predictable, stable environment. Employees, clients, and stakeholders know what to expect and how matters will be handled. This consistency becomes an anchor in turbulent times, helping organizations weather storms of change or crisis.

Consistency Brings Stability

A key benefit of integrity in leadership is the consistency it brings. When leaders are predictable in their principles, their teams and organizations know exactly where they stand. This consistency doesn't mean rigidity; it means that regardless of the external pressures or challenges, your core values remain unchanged. In times of crisis or uncertainty, this provides a source of stability that people can rely on.

In every sector—whether you're leading a small team or an entire company—integrity creates a foundation of trust. It allows leaders to build teams that are not only loyal but also empowered to act with confidence, knowing that their decisions will be supported as long as they align with the organization's values. For example, in corporate environments, leaders who demonstrate unwavering commitment to ethical practices inspire employees to do the same, creating a culture of transparency and accountability.

A Long-Term View of Success

The long-term impact of leading with integrity cannot be overstated. While it might feel challenging in the moment to make the hard decisions, those choices set the stage for enduring success. In both government and the private sector, integrity fosters a reputation that draws respect from colleagues, clients, and competitors alike. Leaders who consistently uphold ethical standards become trusted partners, not only within their organization but also in the broader community.

In leadership, you may not always reap immediate rewards for doing the right thing. In fact, standing on integrity may sometimes come at a personal cost, as I experienced during my tenure as Chief of Police. However, the long-term benefits—trust, respect, and the strength of your character—will pay dividends far beyond any short-term gain.

In my case, pursuing integrity led to difficult times, but it also solidified my commitment to the principles that matter most. And that is true for any leader, in any industry. When you act with integrity, you may face challenges, but in the end, you create a legacy of leadership that others will follow and respect.

Leading with Integrity at Every Level

Leadership with integrity also means being accountable to those you lead. After my reinstatement following a wrongful termination in Simpsonville for standing my ground in the aforementioned situation, I made it my mission to ensure that the department operated with the highest ethical standards. This meant holding officers accountable, providing them with the training they needed to succeed, and fostering a culture where honesty and transparency were valued above all else.

Tough decisions have to be made at the top, and in both of my roles as Chief of Police, I had to hold officers accountable—even those who were well-liked among their peers but who lacked basic principles of integrity. In one instance, I dealt with a top-ranking command staff member who believed it was appropriate to engage in a romantic relationship with a subordinate. When confronted, they denied the relationship, but the favoritism was evident in the workplace and was clearly affecting judgment. Over time, it became impossible to ignore the impact it was having on the department.

Eventually, photographic evidence of the romantic relationship was presented to me by another officer, along with additional evidence that made the case undeniable. I consulted with my boss, the City Administrator, who astonishingly dismissed it as "not a big deal" and stated that he didn't care what people did off duty. I was dumbfounded and suddenly found myself in a position where my ethical standards did not align with those of my superior. I tried to explain that, in law enforcement, someone in a position of power cannot have a romantic relationship with a subordinate and act as though it is consensual, as it could easily lead to claims of coercion or non-consent if the relationship soured.

Despite the City Administrator's indifference, I decided to confront the employee once again. They continued to deny the allegations, but weeks later, they resigned. On their way out, they attempted to create a firestorm of issues to undermine my leadership as Chief of Police but failed to take responsibility for the negative actions that led to their resignation. This individual later moved on to another agency, and the subordinate also left the department.

There are valuable lessons in this story for any leader. This command staff member had been given a second chance by me after being accused of a similar act at another agency. He had vehemently denied the previous accusations, and I wanted to believe in his potential for change. I chose to see the good in him and gave him the opportunity to rise within our department. However, once he achieved a top position, his ego overshadowed his morals, and he compromised himself again. It became clear that if someone shows their true colors, you must believe them. A zebra doesn't change its stripes. Integrity is not something you can teach someone—it is ingrained in a person from a young age.

Some people may float through an organization without facing trouble, motivated only by the fear of consequences. However, once they rise to a top position, the only true guide is their moral compass. Leaders who lack integrity may feel emboldened by their status, believing they can engage in actions that would have previously led to discipline. While they may evade accountability for a time, eventually, their misconduct will catch up to them, and they will have to face the consequences.

The easiest and most honorable path is to always do the right thing. When you lead with integrity, you can move forward confidently, without the burden of looking over your shoulder or fearing the past. In contrast, those who engage in unethical behavior as leaders live like fugitives, constantly wary, never able to fully relax. This is why the old saying rings true: leaders with integrity sleep soundly at night, free from the fear of repercussions for past misdeeds. By choosing to lead ethically, you ensure peace of mind and set a foundation for greater success and fulfillment.

Conclusion: Integrity as the Core of Leadership

In my journey through the ranks of law enforcement, I've learned that integrity is the cornerstone of effective leadership. It's what drives trust, fosters collaboration, and ultimately leads to success. Without it, all the skills, knowledge, and strategies in the world won't make a difference. With it, there's no limit to what can be achieved.

As you read this book, I hope you'll see that every lesson, every story, and every piece of advice is rooted in this fundamental principle: lead with integrity, and everything else will follow. This principle applies to leaders at every level, in every industry. Whether you're guiding a law enforcement agency, leading a corporate team, or serving in public office, integrity will always be the foundation upon which true and lasting success is built.

CHAPTER 1 : LEADING WITH INTEGRITY

Reflect and Apply: Integrity is the cornerstone of effective leadership. As you complete this chapter, reflect on the role integrity plays in your leadership decisions and actions. Think about times when your integrity was tested, and how you responded. Consider the importance of doing the right thing, even when it's difficult or unpopular. To deepen your understanding and apply these lessons, refer to the **Appendix - Leadership Workbook and Action Plans** at the end of the book. Use this section to document your reflections, set personal integrity goals, and explore ways to cultivate a culture of integrity within your team and organization.

CHAPTER 2:

DISCOVERING YOUR LEADERSHIP IDENTITY

Effective leadership begins with self-awareness—understanding who you are as a leader and identifying your unique leadership style. By gaining clarity on how you lead, you can foster deeper growth within yourself and those you lead. Each leader has their own natural tendencies, strengths, and areas for development, and recognizing your leadership style allows you to adapt to various situations and individuals, enhancing your ability to manage diverse teams. While leaders may gravitate toward one particular style, the most well-rounded leaders often embody a combination of approaches, adapting as needed to foster growth, resolve conflicts, and meet organizational goals.

Dynamic Leader: Driving Change and Inspiring Bold Decisions

The Dynamic Leader thrives on energy, innovation, and forward momentum. This leader is not afraid to challenge the status quo and constantly seeks new opportunities for growth and improvement. Dynamic Leaders are often bold decision-makers who take calculated risks and inspire others to embrace change. However, their fast-paced and future-oriented approach can sometimes make it challenging to slow down for reflection or engage in collaborative decision-making.

One of the most powerful tools I used as a Dynamic Leader was painting a clear and exciting vision for the future. My enthusiasm and passion for the direction in which we were heading became contagious, sparking a desire among others to be part of the movement. This infectious energy was instrumental in attracting seasoned, highly qualified law enforcement officers, many of whom were willing to leave higher-ranking positions at larger agencies and even take pay cuts to join our team. These officers saw themselves as contributors to something special and wanted to be part of what they knew would be a success.

When people get excited about a shared vision, they become personally invested in its success. This principle helped me take two police departments that were over 30% understaffed when I arrived and bring them to 100% staffing levels. Not only that, but I also had a waiting list of both uncertified and certified officers eager to join our ranks, just waiting for the right opportunity to become part of the team. Dynamic leadership, with a focus on vision and passion, made all the difference.

But as I grew as a leader, I recognized one of my own weaknesses: I often failed to slow down and celebrate the small wins along the way. My constant focus on the next big challenge meant I was always looking for ways to improve and push forward. While this drive kept me sharp and motivated, it sometimes led me to overlook the value of pausing to recognize the smaller successes.

Growing up with the mindset of always being humble, I found it difficult to outwardly express happiness over a success, especially when others around me had not achieved the same level. This was a reflection of empathy in leadership—a good trait, but one that needs to be balanced. Leaders must find a way to celebrate wins without coming across as arrogant or self-promoting. For me, this has been an area I continue to work on. I realized that celebrating the small victories—both for myself and for the team—builds momentum, boosts morale, and reaffirms that progress is being made.

To address this, I started setting smaller goals within the larger ones. This allowed me to recognize accomplishments along the way, not just at the finish line. It motivated me to keep pushing forward, but more importantly, it gave me the chance to give my team the recognition they deserved. Leadership is about building excitement and passion, but it's also about knowing when to pause, reflect, and celebrate.

As a Dynamic Leader, it's essential to balance your visionary style with moments of reflection and inclusivity. Understanding how your drive for innovation impacts your team allows you to inspire them without overwhelming them. Recognizing and celebrating even the small milestones can ensure that your team stays motivated and connected throughout the journey.

Hands-On Leader: Leading by Example and Staying Engaged

The Hands-On Leader is deeply involved in the day-to-day operations of their team or department. They lead by example, often working side-by-side with their team to demonstrate commitment and dedication. This leadership style is particularly effective in environments that require high levels of accountability and performance. By being closely connected to their team's work, Hands-On Leaders foster strong relationships and build trust.

While this approach can lead to high levels of engagement and productivity, it's important for Hands-On Leaders to avoid micromanagement. A critical aspect of this leadership style is knowing when to step back and trust your team to carry out their responsibilities independently. Great leaders learn to read the situation and understand when their team needs them to be involved and when they need the space to perform. This balance is essential to empowering others and allowing them to take ownership of their roles.

The situation dictates whether a leader should take a hands-on or hands-off approach. For example, in high-pressure, complex scenarios where clear direction is necessary, being hands-on can provide the guidance and stability the team needs. On the other hand, in more routine or developmental situations, stepping back allows team members to grow, develop confidence, and demonstrate their own capabilities. Leaders who master this dynamic are able to inspire trust while fostering greater autonomy among their team members.

Recognizing these moments requires leaders to be highly attuned to their team's mood, capabilities, and needs. When leaders strike the right balance between hands-on engagement and stepping back, they create a positive environment that drives the team forward.

Servant Leader: Prioritizing People, Building Trust, and Righting Wrongs

The Servant Leader prioritizes the well-being and development of their team above all else. This leader focuses on serving others, providing support, and helping their team members grow both personally and professionally. Servant Leaders lead with empathy and compassion, often making decisions based on what is best for their people. This style fosters loyalty, trust, and long-term team engagement.

A story from my own leadership journey illustrates the core principles of Servant Leadership: not being afraid to do the right thing, even when it means revisiting decisions made by others.

When I took over as Chief of Police, I inherited a difficult situation. An officer had been terminated by the previous administration after a shooting incident. Although the shooting was investigated by the state law enforcement division (SLED) and ruled justified, the officer was still fired for alleged policy violations. Despite being cleared of criminal wrongdoing, the officer spent nearly three years outside of law enforcement, fighting to regain his certification and restore his career.

Under South Carolina law, an officer has the right to challenge the loss of their certification for up to three years after an incident. As Chief of Police, it was my responsibility to prosecute any cases of misconduct within my department, including those that occurred before my tenure, if they were brought to a hearing during my time in office. This meant I had to present the facts before the administrative hearing judge.

After reopening the case and conducting a thorough re-investigation, I found significant discrepancies in the previous findings. The officer had been wrongfully targeted by certain command staff members in the prior administration. Four out of the six alleged policy violations were determined to be baseless, while the two remaining violations did not rise to the level of termination. The officer had been treated unfairly, and the termination was unjustified, especially given the officer's clean record of over 10 years of service.

To ensure I was making the right decision, I had two other command staff members independently review the case—both of whom had no prior involvement in the matter. They agreed with my findings. Finally, I gathered the entire command staff to review the evidence and discuss the case, and we reached a consensus: the officer had been wrongfully terminated.

Despite pressure from one command staff member—who had been involved in the original decision to terminate the officer—to leave the matter alone, I knew I had to act. Servant Leadership is about doing what is right for your people, even when it's difficult. There is no gray area when it comes to right and wrong.

During the officer's hearing, I took the stand and presented my findings on the record. Both the officer's attorney and the administrative judge remarked that they had never seen a Chief of Police admit to errors and work to correct a wrong of this magnitude. It was disheartening to learn that this kind of intervention was rare, but I was proud to stand up for justice and ensure that an innocent officer wasn't wrongfully blackballed from the profession.

Soon after the hearing, the officer's law enforcement certification was reinstated, making them eligible to return to duty, though they did not have a job at the time. When I later received a call from another law enforcement agency asking for a recommendation, I told them the truth: the officer had been wrongfully terminated, had proven their integrity, and had my full support. The officer was hired and has since continued to excel in their law enforcement career.

This experience wasn't about taking the easy road or avoiding difficult decisions—it was about standing up for justice, even when it meant admitting mistakes from the past. As a Servant Leader, I had a responsibility not only to my department but also to the individual officers who relied on me to ensure fairness.

Just as in law enforcement, Servant Leadership is a powerful model for the private sector. In the corporate world, leaders who prioritize their team's development and well-being build stronger, more loyal, and engaged employees. By fostering trust and ensuring fairness, leaders can create a culture where people are empowered to succeed. And, as seen in this story, even tough decisions that go against the grain can have a long-lasting positive impact on team morale and overall organizational success.

Strategic Leader: Thinking Long-Term and Making Informed Decisions

The Strategic Leader takes a big-picture view, focusing on long-term goals and ensuring that short-term actions align with the broader mission. These leaders excel at analyzing data, identifying trends, and crafting clear plans for the future. Their analytical approach helps them navigate complex challenges and anticipate future needs, positioning the organization for success.

While Strategic Leaders are excellent planners, they need to be mindful of staying connected to their team's daily realities. Combining their strategic focus with the human element ensures they remain grounded in the practical aspects of leadership while steering the team toward long-term success.

Collaborative Leader: Fostering Teamwork and Inclusivity

The Collaborative Leader emphasizes teamwork, inclusivity, and shared decision-making. They believe that the best solutions come from diverse perspectives and open dialogue. Collaborative Leaders actively seek input from their teams and create environments where everyone feels empowered to contribute. This leadership style builds a culture of trust, transparency, and shared responsibility.

While collaboration is a powerful tool for fostering innovation, Collaborative Leaders must ensure that decisions are still made efficiently. Striking the right balance between inclusivity and decisiveness is essential for driving the team forward.

Authoritative Leader: Fostering Teamwork and Inclusivity

The Authoritative Leader is confident and assertive, setting clear direction and expectations. They lead with a strong vision and provide decisive leadership, which is especially effective during times of crisis or uncertainty. Authoritative Leaders inspire respect through their clear communication, confidence, and ability to navigate high-pressure situations.

However, Authoritative Leaders need to be cautious of becoming too rigid. While decisiveness is important, listening to feedback and adjusting plans as needed will help create a more balanced leadership style that fosters team buy-in and trust. A lack of flexibility can cause friction within the team, especially when different personalities or evolving circumstances require a more adaptable approach.

A real-world example from my own leadership experience illustrates this point. While serving as Chief of Police, I promoted a Captain to the rank of Major. This individual was highly respected for their tactical expertise and authoritative command, a style that had served them well in the field. Unfortunately, they had advanced through the ranks relatively quickly and had not spent enough time in more intermediate leadership roles, such as Captain and Lieutenant, to fully develop a diverse leadership approach.

One of the Major's greatest strengths was his ability to make quick, confident decisions—an authoritative approach that proved invaluable in high-stress, tactical situations. However, this leadership style became problematic when applied to broader command staff responsibilities. The Major struggled to transition from the fast-paced, rigid decision-making required in a field Sergeant or tactical team lead role to the more nuanced and collaborative leadership style necessary for overseeing a large department with a diverse team of individuals.

I worked closely with the Major, holding mentoring sessions to help them understand the importance of flexibility and adaptability in leadership. While their authoritative approach had been effective in high-stakes, tactical environments, they needed to develop the ability to switch gears and be more collaborative and inclusive in their new role. It wasn't always about barking commands or being rigid, and the Major had difficulty breaking out of that "field sergeant mindset."

Despite my efforts, the Major couldn't adjust their leadership style to meet the needs of the broader command staff and department. This led to significant clashes between us, as well as with other members of the leadership team. The inability to adapt created an environment of friction, where trust and collaboration were eroded. Ultimately, it became clear that their rigid approach was negatively affecting the organization, and it was in the best interest of the department for the Major to move on to another agency.

This experience taught me a valuable lesson: while the authoritative leadership style has its place, especially in crisis situations, it is crucial for leaders to be able to adapt their approach based on the needs of their team and the context of the situation. As you move higher up in an organization, the need to develop an array of different leadership skills becomes increasingly important. The higher you rise, the more you must navigate the balance between decisive leadership and fostering an inclusive, collaborative environment.

Your people need to know that you genuinely care about them, and if you maintain an authoritative stance at all times, it can create an impersonal atmosphere, particularly in an administrative role. This can make you seem unapproachable, leading to a lack of trust within the team. When leaders are seen as unapproachable, those under them may withhold valuable ideas or innovative approaches out of fear or hesitation. In the long run, this stifles creativity and limits the organization's ability to grow and improve. Great leaders understand when to be authoritative and when to step back, listen, and empower their team. By showing empathy and approachability, you foster a culture of trust and innovation.

Great leadership is about balance—knowing when to lead from the front and when to lead from behind, allowing others to step up and take responsibility. The failure to adjust one's leadership style can ultimately hinder both the leader and the team's success.

Innovative Leader: Embracing Change and Encouraging Creativity

The Innovative Leader is constantly evolving, always seeking new ideas, approaches, and technologies to keep themselves and their organization relevant. What sets an Innovative Leader apart is their willingness to try new things and listen to the ideas of others, fostering a culture of creativity and adaptability. They are forward-thinking, often seeing opportunities where others see obstacles. This leadership style thrives in environments where change is frequent, and the ability to adapt is critical for success.

Innovative Leaders are not afraid to experiment and take risks. They understand that with innovation comes occasional failure, but they view these setbacks as opportunities to learn and improve. By encouraging their teams to think outside the box, these leaders create a safe space for creativity to flourish, empowering individuals to share bold ideas without fear of judgment. This approach not only drives the organization forward but also helps foster a growth mindset within the team.

One of the hallmarks of an Innovative Leader is their openness to feedback. They actively seek input from others, recognizing that the best solutions often come from diverse perspectives. Whether it's incorporating feedback from frontline employees or adopting suggestions from different departments, Innovative Leaders build an environment where continuous improvement is a shared goal. By staying open to new ideas and technologies, they ensure that their team remains competitive and resilient in the face of change.

However, it's essential for Innovative Leaders to balance their enthusiasm for new ideas with practicality. While it's important to experiment, they must also ensure that resources are used wisely and that innovation aligns with the organization's overall mission and goals.

Adaptive Leader: Flexibility in the Face of Change

The Adaptive Leader is flexible, adjusting their approach to meet the needs of their team and the situation at hand. They thrive in dynamic environments and are comfortable navigating change. Adaptive Leaders are skilled at reading the room and adapting their leadership style to align with the moment, whether that means stepping up as a hands-on guide or stepping back to let others take the lead.

The strength of the Adaptive Leader is their ability to be a chameleon in leadership, pulling from various styles to suit different challenges. However, it's important for Adaptive Leaders to maintain a core set of principles and values, ensuring that flexibility doesn't lead to inconsistency.

Blending Leadership Styles for Success

The most effective leaders recognize that they are not confined to one particular leadership style. While you may naturally gravitate toward one approach, being a well-rounded leader often means blending different styles depending on the situation. For example, you may adopt a Hands-On approach when your team needs direct support, shift to Strategic Leadership when setting long-term goals, and embrace Servant Leadership when focusing on team development.

Understanding your natural leadership tendencies allows you to identify areas where you can grow and become more versatile. Combining leadership styles gives you the flexibility to meet the needs of your team while driving organizational success. The key is to be self-aware—understanding how you naturally lead—and adaptable enough to switch styles as needed for the good of the team and the organization.

Getting to Know Yourself as a Leader

The foundation of great leadership starts with knowing yourself. Take the time to reflect on your leadership tendencies and how they influence your team. Consider past leadership experiences and identify which styles have worked best for you in different situations. Being honest about your strengths and areas for growth is the first step to becoming a more effective, well-rounded leader.

Self-awareness not only helps you lead better but also allows you to understand how you react to different types of people. By knowing yourself, you can better manage diverse personalities, resolve conflicts, and foster a team culture that values collaboration, empathy, and accountability. Whether you're naturally a Dynamic Leader, an Innovative Leader, or somewhere in between, understanding your unique leadership identity will help you foster deeper connections, lead with confidence, and adapt to any situation that comes your way.

CHAPTER 2 : DISCOVERING YOUR LEADERSHIP IDENTITY

Reflect and Apply: Understanding your leadership style is key to leading effectively. Take some time to reflect on your own leadership identity. Are you a servant leader, strategic thinker, or a combination of styles? Turn to the **Appendix - Leadership Workbook and Action Plans** to document your leadership strengths, identify areas for growth, and set actionable goals for enhancing your leadership approach.

CHAPTER 3:

PROACTIVE LEADERSHIP: A PATH TO SUCCESS

The greatest leaders in history share one common trait: they are proactive. Rather than waiting for problems to escalate, they anticipate challenges and address them before they become unmanageable. This trait is a key differentiator between great leaders and reactive managers. Whether in law enforcement, the private sector, or any other organizational environment, proactive leadership is essential for long-term success. It ensures not only the safety and well-being of those under your leadership but also increases efficiency, prevents crises, and reduces costs. Organizations that foster a proactive mindset at every level are far more likely to thrive.

A prime example of proactive leadership can be seen in both law enforcement and corporate environments. A law enforcement leader who preemptively increases patrols in high-crime areas or creates community programs to deter criminal activity is much more effective than one who merely responds to calls. Similarly, in the private sector, companies that consistently monitor market trends, customer behavior, and internal processes are better equipped to pivot when necessary.

Leaders who can recognize and respond to early signals of change are the ones who sustain organizational growth and success over time.

Consider a company that consistently monitors emerging technologies, such as AI. By proactively investing in artificial intelligence, the company anticipates future industry demands and avoids falling behind competitors. In contrast, a company that waits until AI becomes mainstream may struggle to keep up, scrambling to retrofit processes and losing ground to companies that embraced proactive leadership early on.

The Link Between Procrastination and Reactive Leadership

Procrastination and reactive leadership are closely connected. A leader who constantly puts off tasks and decisions is more likely to react to problems after they arise instead of preventing them. This reactive approach can lead to crises, inefficiency, and missed opportunities. On the surface, some individuals may appear proactive by making last-minute decisions or appearing busy, but this façade is unsustainable. Maintaining true proactivity requires consistent effort, foresight, and self-discipline. Genuine proactive leaders are internally driven to stay ahead, continuously improve, and never allow problems to catch them off guard.

For me, this motivation stems from a desire to always be the best or, at the very least, better than I was before. I've seen firsthand how this drive can sometimes provoke jealousy or resentment from others who aren't as driven. People may talk behind your back because you're doing what they cannot or are unwilling to do. But the reality is, proactive leadership requires a constant commitment to improvement and foresight. In both law enforcement and business environments, leaders who can effectively plan ahead are seen as catalysts for progress.

In the corporate world, procrastination can have devastating effects on a company's trajectory. For instance, imagine a CEO who delays critical decisions about launching a new product or restructuring a failing department. These delays may seem harmless in the short term, but over time, they cause the company to lose its competitive edge, waste valuable resources, and weaken relationships with customers. By the time the CEO reacts, it may already be too late, and the company is left scrambling to recover. This cycle of reactionary decision-making leaves organizations vulnerable to market forces, competitors, and internal inefficiencies.

The History of Reactive Policing

Traditionally, policing has been a reactive profession. For centuries, officers responded to crimes after they occurred, addressing immediate threats but rarely getting ahead of them. While this reactive approach is sometimes necessary, relying on it exclusively leaves communities vulnerable. Officers are often seen as responders to crises rather than protectors who actively work to prevent crime. Yet, within every department, some officers stand out for their proactive efforts. These are the officers who look beyond the immediate crisis and work to prevent future issues. This proactive mindset must be cultivated and encouraged by leadership, ensuring that departments blend reactive responsibilities with proactive strategies.

One key example of proactive versus reactive leadership can be seen immediately after natural disasters, such as hurricanes or severe weather events. Ideally, we aim to mitigate the impact of these events by providing timely information, coordinating evacuations, strategically placing sandbags, or stockpiling clean water and other essential supplies. In cases where these preparatory actions are taken, proactive leaders can still take additional measures to prevent further harm immediately after a natural disaster.

For instance, if a tree is down on a road and cannot be removed right away, police can set up cones or barricades to warn motorists. Additionally, they can notify the public via social media, alerting them to the hazard and helping prevent accidents. Another key preparation involves ensuring access to shelters and designating drop-off and pick-up locations for essential supplies. Proactively setting up these locations ahead of time can make all the difference in the aftermath, as people in need of shelter and supplies can be quickly accommodated, reducing chaos and confusion.

I have witnessed both effective and ineffective responses to such situations. Jurisdictions that failed to act often placed their community at risk, creating liability due to inaction, potentially leading to death or serious injury. Failing to warn the public of a known hazard—or one that could be identified through proactive patrols—is negligent. Proactivity is about addressing small details and acting before a catastrophe occurs.

In the business world, this same principle applies. Imagine a manufacturing company with a history of equipment malfunctions. A reactive approach waits for a machine to break down before fixing it, halting production and causing delays. A proactive approach, however, implements routine maintenance schedules and invests in newer, more efficient machinery before breakdowns occur. This not only saves time and resources but also ensures the company operates smoothly, without interruptions. In both law enforcement and corporate sectors, proactive leadership allows organizations to operate efficiently while minimizing risks and disruptions.

For example, if you expect heavy rain and know that a certain river always overflows and causes road closures, a proactive leader would shut down the road early and notify the public. This simple action can prevent someone from entering fast-moving waters and requiring a dangerous swift water rescue, which could endanger even more lives. The recognition you receive for these preventative measures may not be obvious because, by preventing something, it never happens. But it is a crucial part of ensuring public safety, and great leaders understand the importance of taking these preemptive actions.

In the corporate world, this could be akin to a product manager foreseeing a shift in consumer preferences and adjusting the company's product lineup before sales dip. This leader may not get immediate recognition for avoiding a potential disaster, but their foresight keeps the company ahead of the curve.

A Case for Proactive Police Work

As a specific example from my time as Chief of Police, we adopted a fully proactive policing strategy to combat rising drug crimes in our community. Every member of the department was trained in basic drug investigations and identification, enabling them to recognize indicators of more severe offenses, such as drug trafficking or distribution, rather than just possession. This comprehensive training gave officers the tools to dig deeper into potential criminal activities rather than simply responding to them.

Additionally, we offered every individual arrested on a drug-related offense the opportunity to become an informant. This proactive strategy allowed us to gather more intelligence on higher-level criminal activities and disrupt drug distribution networks. Beyond that, we invested in community-based programs to build public trust. These initiatives encouraged more citizens to submit anonymous tips, greatly enhancing our ability to detect and prevent crime.

The results were profound. Our department increased drug arrests and detected drug crimes by over 287%. This surge in proactive policing not only led to a safer community but also improved the city's safety ranking, propelling it from the 28th safest city in South Carolina to the number one spot. There is only one number one, and for a city that had previously not even been in the top 25, this achievement was a testament to the power of proactive leadership. Unfortunately, after my departure and the shift back to more reactive policing methods, the city no longer remains in the top 20, underscoring the direct impact that proactive strategies can have on community safety.

In the private sector, the lessons from this approach are equally applicable. For instance, consider a retail chain that notices increased thefts in certain stores. A proactive approach would involve not only increasing security measures but also addressing underlying causes—such as poor store layout, inadequate staffing, or even social factors in the area. By engaging employees in theft prevention training and implementing early interventions, such as security cameras or floor staff placement, the company could significantly reduce losses and improve overall operations. It's about recognizing patterns, understanding vulnerabilities, and addressing them before they become full-blown crises.

The Role of Servant Leadership in Proactive Leadership

Leaders should never forget where they come from as they climb the ranks or achieve greatness. This does not make them better than anyone else; in fact, the higher up you go, the greater servant you must be for your people. True leadership is not about sitting in an office while others do the work. It is about being in the trenches with your team, understanding their challenges, and providing the support they need to succeed.

In law enforcement, servant leadership means prioritizing the well-being of both your officers and the community. It means equipping officers with the skills and resources to not only respond to crime but also to prevent it. It means being proactive in addressing issues within the department, ensuring that officers are well-trained, supported, and motivated to do their best work.

In the private sector, servant leadership plays a similar role. Leaders who prioritize their employees' growth and well-being are much more likely to foster a proactive culture within the organization. For example, a CEO who invests in employee development, listens to concerns, and takes steps to create a supportive work environment will see that employees are more engaged, innovative, and willing to go the extra mile. This engagement directly translates into proactive thinking—when employees feel valued and empowered, they are more likely to identify problems early and suggest creative solutions.

In both settings, servant leaders stay connected to their people, which enables them to make better, more informed decisions. When employees trust their leaders and feel supported, they are more inclined to bring forward issues before they escalate. This builds a culture of proactivity where everyone is aligned in their commitment to improvement and growth.

Conclusion: Proactive Leadership is Key to Success

Proactive leadership, whether in policing or the private sector, is essential for long-term success. It builds trust, prevents crises, and ensures that organizations are not constantly reacting to problems but staying ahead of them. For leaders willing to put in the effort, the rewards are immense: safer communities, improved morale, lower costs, and stronger reputations for excellence.

In law enforcement, the importance of proactive leadership cannot be overstated. It allows departments to reduce crime, increase public safety, and build trust within the community. More importantly, it shifts the perception of law enforcement from being merely reactive—responding to calls and investigating crimes—to being a forward-thinking entity that actively works to prevent crimes before they happen.

In the private sector, the same principles apply. Proactive business leaders don't wait for sales to drop before revising their marketing strategies. They don't wait for equipment to break before initiating maintenance protocols. They anticipate problems, prepare for them, and take preemptive action to avoid costly errors. A company that monitors industry trends, customer feedback, and internal performance data is far more likely to succeed in the long run. Businesses led by proactive individuals avoid disruptions, cultivate innovation, and can seize market opportunities before their competitors even realize there's a gap.

For example, imagine a retail company that notices a steady decline in foot traffic in certain locations. A reactive approach would be to wait until profits plummet and then close the stores. A proactive leader, however, might identify the issue early and take steps to address it. They could diversify their product offerings, increase marketing in those areas, or pivot toward online sales. By recognizing potential problems before they manifest, the company not only avoids a financial crisis but also positions itself for long-term growth.

Proactive leadership also boosts employee morale and engagement. Employees in an organization led by proactive leaders are more likely to feel valued and heard. They understand that their leaders are looking out for their well-being, not just reacting to crises but taking deliberate steps to improve the workplace and foster their professional growth. In the private sector, this can lead to better retention, increased productivity, and a culture of innovation where everyone feels empowered to contribute solutions rather than simply following orders.

Ultimately, being proactive isn't just a leadership strategy—it's a mindset. It's about anticipating challenges, preparing for them, and maintaining a forward-thinking approach at all times. Whether you're leading a police department, managing a team in a corporate office, or running your own business, proactive leadership is the foundation of long-term success. The rewards may not always be immediately visible, but the difference it makes—whether in the form of lower crime rates, higher profits, or happier employees—will become clear over time.

CHAPTER 3 : PROACTIVE LEADERSHIP: A PATH TO SUCCESS

Reflect and Apply: Proactive leadership is essential to staying ahead of challenges and driving long-term success, whether in law enforcement or the private sector. Reflect on how often you take proactive steps versus reacting to problems as they arise. Are you creating a forward-thinking environment where your team or organization anticipates obstacles and addresses them early? Turn to the **Appendix - Leadership Workbook and Action Plans** to outline your proactive strategies. Document specific steps to enhance foresight and take preemptive action in your leadership. Identify key areas where you can build a more proactive mindset within your team, ensuring you remain ahead of the curve in preventing issues and fostering growth.

CHAPTER 4:

CRISIS MANAGEMENT

Crisis management is a test of a leader's ability to stay calm under pressure, make quick decisions, and guide their team through challenging situations. Throughout my career in law enforcement, I've faced numerous crises—both on the streets of cities across the U.S. and in volatile regions abroad—that have taught me the importance of being prepared, decisive, and resilient.

One of the most significant lessons I learned about crisis management came during my time as the U.S. Contingent Commander in Haiti, working on a U.S. Department of State mission with the United Nations. The country was plagued by violence, drug trafficking, extreme poverty and political instability. As the leader responsible for U.S. police advisors and foreign contingents of police specializing in Special Weapons and Tactics (SWAT) and nationwide Crowd Control responses of designated Formed Police Units (FPUs), I had to quickly adapt to the complexities of the situation. There was no room for hesitation; lives were at stake, and real crises occurred daily. In Haiti, every decision had to be made with both immediate and long-term consequences in mind.

The experience underscored the importance of preparation. A leader must anticipate potential crises and have a plan in place to address them. This means conducting thorough risk assessments, training your team to respond effectively, and ensuring that everyone knows their role when things go wrong. In Haiti, we had to prepare for everything from natural disasters (earthquakes and hurricanes) to coordinated attacks by criminal gangs. Our success depended on our ability to think ahead and remain flexible in our approach.

Another critical aspect of crisis management is communication. During a crisis, clear and consistent communication is essential to maintaining order and ensuring that everyone is on the same page. In Haiti, I had to coordinate with various stakeholders, including local law enforcement, the U.S. Embassy, and international organizations. This required not only a clear understanding of the situation but also the ability to convey that understanding to others in a way that inspired confidence and cooperation throughout more than 500 operations over a two year period.

Leadership in Liberia During the COVID-19 Pandemic

One of the most impactful leadership lessons I learned came during my time in Liberia, West Africa, when the COVID-19 pandemic hit. At the time, I was serving as the Senior Law Enforcement Advisor to the Inspector General of Police, who had been appointed by the Liberian President and was responsible for all police and security forces across the nation. Liberia, a country already struggling with poverty, lacked the infrastructure and medical resources to handle a widespread pandemic, making the situation particularly dire.

We knew that preparing for a response to an unknown disease like COVID-19 would be critical, especially in a nation that did not have a single functioning respirator. A COVID-19 diagnosis was essentially a death sentence due to the lack of adequate medical care. Recognizing the gravity of the situation, I collaborated with the Inspector General and other national leaders to create a strategic plan for preventing the widespread transmission of the virus.

We began by examining Liberia's history, particularly its experience with the Ebola outbreak years earlier. The country still had access to hand-washing stations, digital touchless thermometers, and other resources used during the Ebola crisis. In addition, we had just received dozens of megaphones for a crowd control communication project. These resources, though minimal, became the backbone of our public awareness campaign.

We used the megaphones to spread COVID-19 safety messages in communities that lacked electricity, driving through villages and holding community meetings to ensure the public understood the risks and preventive measures. We set up hand-washing stations across the country, worked with local producers to manufacture face masks, and implemented safety measures to slow the spread of the virus. By focusing on education and prevention, we managed to slow the spread of COVID-19 significantly, making Liberia one of the last nations in the region to experience widespread transmission.

This experience taught me invaluable lessons about leadership during a crisis: adaptability, resourcefulness, and communication were key. Leading a country with limited resources through a global pandemic highlighted the importance of using whatever tools are available to protect your team and the people you serve. Whether in law enforcement or corporate settings, crisis management requires leaders to think outside the box, communicate effectively, and be proactive in their response.

Lessons for Crisis Management in the Business World

The leadership lessons I learned in Liberia and other crisis situations have broad applications in the business world. Crisis management in any organization—whether responding to a pandemic, a financial downturn, or internal organizational challenges—demands a leader who can remain calm, decisive, and forward-thinking.

In Liberia, we were working with limited resources, but the principles we applied are relevant in any industry. Preparation is crucial. Just as we leveraged Liberia's past experience with Ebola to inform our COVID-19 response, businesses must look at historical data and previous challenges to anticipate future crises. Having contingency plans in place and being able to pivot when the unexpected happens can make the difference between failure and survival.

Communication is equally essential in business. During a crisis, the workforce and stakeholders will look to leadership for direction and reassurance. Leaders must provide clear, consistent messaging that keeps everyone aligned and focused on the goals ahead. In Liberia, we communicated directly with the public using simple, effective methods like megaphones in communities without electricity. In business, leaders must adapt their communication strategies to reach all employees, from remote workers to international teams, ensuring that everyone understands the plan and their role in it.

Furthermore, crisis management requires adaptability and the ability to make the best use of available resources. Whether it's leveraging megaphones in Liberia or reallocating a company's resources in a financial crisis, successful leadership often means finding creative solutions to unprecedented challenges. In a corporate setting, this could involve repurposing staff, rethinking product lines, or finding new ways to serve customers when usual operations are disrupted.

Lastly, crises provide an opportunity to reinforce the core values of leadership. Just as I remained committed to public health in Liberia despite the overwhelming odds, business leaders must maintain their commitment to ethics, transparency, and accountability during tough times. A well-managed crisis can strengthen an organization's reputation and build trust with both employees and stakeholders.

Crisis Management in Law Enforcement and Beyond

In the United States, while working as a Special Agent with the U.S. Drug Enforcement Administration (DEA), I applied these lessons during my tenure as co-commander of a violent crime/drug task force spanning 36 counties across western Kansas. One particular crisis stands out and was the reason we formed this task force. We faced a surge in gang activity that threatened the safety of our communities. The situation required immediate action, but it also required careful planning and coordination. We implemented a multi-agency task force, involving the local sheriff's departments, state police, and municipal police departments. My role was to ensure that all parties were working together effectively, that we communicated our strategy clearly to the public, and that we made a tangible impact on reducing gang activity, drug trafficking, violence, and other related crimes.

One of the key elements of managing this task force was conducting post-incident debriefings, similar to what we did with our SWAT teams in Haiti or the High-Risk Narcotics Entry Teams I served on in the United States. These debriefings were crucial because they forced us to check our egos at the door and candidly discuss the challenges we encountered during operations. We had to openly examine what went right, what went wrong, and how we could improve our approach for the next operation. This honest reflection was not only vital for short-term tactical missions but also for long-term strategic planning.

For example, I recall a significant shortcoming we failed to anticipate during our gang task force operations—the local impact we would make on jail populations. After a massive sting operation where we made 96 arrests in the first 12 hours, we received complaints from a particular sheriff in western Kansas about overcrowding in his jail. This was not a complaint we expected, especially since this same sheriff had been vocal about the gang problem in his jurisdiction. The issue highlighted a blind spot in our planning: while we had focused heavily on executing the sting successfully, we hadn't fully accounted for the logistical and resource burdens it would place on the local jail system.

This lesson underscored the importance of considering all potential consequences of an operation, not just the immediate tactical goals. In crisis management, whether you're working on short-term tactical missions or long-term projects, you must be ready to address unintended impacts and make adjustments accordingly. These debriefings and reflections are essential in identifying those gaps and ensuring future operations run more smoothly.

Finally, a key element of crisis management is the ability to learn from every experience. After each operation, we conducted thorough reviews to evaluate what worked, what didn't, and where we could improve. This process of reflection is not only critical in law enforcement but is also essential in any organization. In Kansas, after we reduced gang activity, we didn't just celebrate the success—we took a step back to assess the broader impact, including unforeseen consequences like the strain on local jail populations. This level of analysis is important in the corporate world as well. Whether launching a new product, completing a major project, or navigating a crisis, leaders must take the time to review outcomes, address any gaps, and implement adjustments for future endeavors.

In both law enforcement and business, the ability to evaluate and adapt based on past performance is what separates good leaders from great ones. It's not enough to simply complete a task successfully—you must also reflect on the process, learn from the challenges, and refine your approach for the future. This mindset fosters continuous improvement and ensures that each crisis or project becomes a stepping stone for greater efficiency and success down the road.

Conclusion: Leadership in Crisis

Crisis management is never easy, but it's a critical part of leadership. The ability to navigate a crisis effectively can make the difference between success and failure. Whether you're dealing with a natural disaster, a public safety threat, or a crisis within your organization, the principles remain the same: be prepared, communicate clearly, stay calm, and learn from every experience.

As you continue to develop your leadership skills, remember that crises are opportunities to demonstrate your strength as a leader. They are the moments when your team needs you the most, and how you respond will define your leadership for years to come.

CHAPTER 4 : CRISIS MANAGEMENT

Reflect and Apply: Crisis tests leadership like nothing else. Reflect on how you've managed crises in the past and how you can improve for future challenges. For a deeper exploration, go to the **Appendix - Leadership Workbook and Action Plans** and outline your crisis management strategies, ensuring that you're prepared to lead effectively when it matters most.

CHAPTER 5:

BUILDING AND LEADING EFFECTIVE TEAMS

A leader's success is not just measured by individual achievements but by the strength, cohesion, and effectiveness of the team they lead. Throughout my career in law enforcement, I've witnessed how crucial it is to build a team that is skilled, united by a shared purpose, and empowered to take ownership of their roles. The successes we achieved in my previous leadership roles were not the work of one person but the outcome of collective effort, driven by trust, communication, and mutual respect.

When I first stepped into a Police Chief leadership role, the department needed more than just new policies or strategies—it needed a cultural shift. The department was struggling with low morale, internal conflicts, and a lack of direction. My first priority was to listen to the concerns of the officers and understand the team dynamics. I held a series of one-on-one meetings with every member of the department, from the newest recruits to the most senior officers. These conversations were revealing. Not only did they highlight the challenges we faced, but they also unveiled the untapped potential within the team.

Trust as the Foundation

Building an effective team starts with trust. As a leader, it's essential to establish an environment where your team members feel valued, heard, and supported. Trust is earned through consistent actions, honesty, and transparency. In my leadership role, I made it clear that my door was always open and that I was just as committed to the well-being of the officers as I was to the success of our mission. This openness built a foundation of trust, which became the bedrock of our team's strength.

However, operating an open-door policy requires clear boundaries. I emphasized that before coming directly to me, employees should attempt to resolve issues with their supervisors or peers. If they were unable to find a resolution, they were welcome to bring the problem to me—along with three possible solutions. Additionally, I asked that concerns be submitted in writing. This not only provided a "cooling-off" period to prevent heated exchanges but also helped clarify the issues and focus on solutions. This strategy can be applied in any organization—whether a police department or a corporate office—where fostering self-sufficiency and problem-solving capabilities is essential for growth.

Communication as a Critical Component

Communication is the lifeblood of any successful team. In my leadership roles, I prioritized regular communication through briefings, team meetings, and informal check-ins. This allowed everyone to stay on the same page and ensured that roles and responsibilities were clear. Frequent communication also created space for sharing ideas and concerns, strengthening our collective problem-solving capabilities. In corporate settings, regular communication is equally critical, especially as teams navigate complex projects or shifting priorities.

One of the most valuable lessons I learned about communication came from my international experiences, where I led U.S. police advisors in Haiti, Afghanistan, and Liberia. Bridging cultural differences, navigating foreign legal frameworks, and managing diverse teams taught me that open communication is essential for collaboration. In these environments, mutual respect and the willingness to listen allowed our teams to rely on each other's strengths. The corporate world can also draw from this lesson. Diverse teams with varied backgrounds and perspectives can be a powerful asset—when communication is open and clear, innovation and collaboration thrive.

Accountability as a Pillar

Accountability is a cornerstone of effective leadership. Every team member must understand their responsibilities and be held accountable for their actions. However, this doesn't mean ruling with an iron fist; it means setting clear expectations and providing the support necessary to meet them. In my leadership roles, I implemented a system of regular performance evaluations and feedback sessions, which kept us aligned with our goals and allowed for continuous improvement. I also asked my command staff to hold me accountable for my actions and promises—a practice that ensured a culture of mutual responsibility.

Positive reinforcement is equally essential. When an employee goes beyond what is expected, recognizing their efforts formally is crucial. The greater the accomplishment, the more important it is to reward the behavior. This positive reinforcement sends a clear message that excellence and going the extra mile are valued and will result in positive outcomes. Acknowledging and rewarding such behavior encourages others to follow suit, contributing to a culture of excellence.

On the other hand, negative actions that undermine public trust or do not align with the values of the organization must be addressed. I am a firm believer in progressive discipline, ensuring that individuals are held accountable in a fair and transparent manner. Failing to hold employees accountable for detrimental actions sends mixed messages that such behavior is tolerable. This can undermine the direction and standards you are trying to set for the department.

In corporate environments, accountability is just as vital. A high-performing team is one where every member understands their role and feels empowered to take ownership of their work. Regular check-ins, feedback loops, and performance reviews provide a structured way to reinforce accountability while fostering growth. Combining this approach with positive reinforcement for exceptional performance and appropriate consequences for negative actions creates a balanced and thriving organizational culture.

Empowering Your Team

Leadership isn't about doing everything yourself; it's about empowering others to step into leadership roles. One effective way to encourage your team to take ownership is by giving them the responsibility to manage their own projects. As Chief of Police, I fostered this by requiring each shift in Uniform Patrol to create and oversee an annual project. This initiative empowered sergeants to lead while engaging the entire team in a collaborative effort.

Each shift presented their project ideas to me for approval, and once approved, they were responsible for executing the plan and securing any necessary funding. Some teams sought local sponsors, while others organized fundraisers, showcasing creativity, innovation, and dedication to the community. One standout project was an autism awareness program initiated by a shift that included an officer with a child on the autism spectrum. This program not only trained officers on how to interact with individuals with autism but also generated positive feedback from the community.

Empowering my team extended beyond projects; it was reflected in the decisions I made regarding their equipment. When I first became Chief, I discovered that our patrol fleet was in dire condition—the majority of uniform patrol vehicles had over 100,000 miles and visible rust. Meanwhile, the Assistant Chief and I had been provided brand-new Chevy Chargers, fully outfitted with high-performance patrol packages.

These flashy cars, more suited for a *Fast and Furious* movie, were not what the department leadership needed most.

To demonstrate that I prioritized my officers, I took my keys and the keys from my Assistant Chief and handed them to the two top-performing sergeants on Uniform Patrol, telling them the cars were theirs to distribute as they saw fit. This decision was a hidden test to see if they would keep the cars or give them to their best-performing officers. They passed, giving the cars to their most productive team members, which immediately earned them respect from the ranks. From that day on, I drove an old Crown Vic and vowed not to get a new car until the entire fleet had been replaced. By the time I left, the fleet had been fully upgraded, though I never received a new vehicle myself.

This act of selflessness and commitment to my team's needs not only empowered my officers but also instilled a sense of trust and loyalty. It demonstrated that leadership is about ensuring your team has the tools to succeed, even if it means sacrificing your own comforts.

Corporate leaders can draw valuable lessons from these examples. When team members feel empowered to take ownership of projects and are trusted with important decisions, they become more engaged, resourceful, and committed to the organization's goals. Empowering your team builds independence, creativity, and resilience—qualities that are essential for overcoming challenges and ensuring long-term success.

The Power of Motivation in Leadership

The best way to motivate people is to hire or surround yourself with motivated individuals. Leaders are self-motivated individuals, and great leaders not only possess internal drive but also have the ability to inspire and motivate others. Inspiring people is a skill set that requires intentional effort and self-reflection. As a leader, you must determine what fuels and drives you to do more.

For me, I am driven by seeking greatness and proving others wrong. I remember as a young police officer, encountering individuals who had a negative perception of law enforcement. I took it upon myself to change their mindset by showing them that police officers are regular people, not superheroes, who strive to do their best and learn from every situation. This approach helped me connect with people and challenge stereotypes, and it stuck with me throughout my career.

As I gained experience, I became more cynical at times, but I never gave up on the dream of showing those who may not appreciate or respect law enforcement that we are just like them. We all make mistakes, and we all bleed. The ability to motivate others comes from a place of authenticity, and it starts with understanding what drives you to lead and inspire others.

Motivation is contagious. Surrounding yourself with people who are driven creates an environment of high energy and purpose. This not only applies to your team but also to those who support you in your personal and professional life. In leadership, motivation is key to cultivating a culture where people are excited to contribute, innovate, and collaborate for a common goal.

The Employee Action Committee: Giving the Team a Voice

One way I fostered empowerment and open communication in law enforcement was through the creation of the Employee Action Committee (EAC) in each department I led. The EAC provided a platform for non-ranking representatives from each division—such as patrol, records, detectives, and others—to meet directly with me once per month, without the presence of higher-ranking officers. This unique setup ensured that the "boots on the ground" workers had an uninterrupted channel to voice their concerns, suggestions, and solutions directly to the top leader.

In many paramilitary organizations with a rigid rank structure, issues often rise through the chain of command but stall at certain levels—such as the Captain or Lieutenant level—for various reasons, including personal bias or unwillingness to address certain problems. This can lead to a disconnect between the leadership at the top and the workers on the front lines. Leaders can be left unaware of real issues affecting their teams, which in turn can make them appear out of touch and unresponsive. The EAC eliminated this barrier by bypassing the typical rank structure, allowing employees to communicate candidly without fear of reprisal or filtering of information.

This direct access to leadership was critical for ensuring that I remained informed of the real challenges and concerns affecting my team. It allowed me to identify problems that were not being addressed by my own command staff and hold them accountable for their responsibilities. Initially, some of my command staff members were resistant to the idea, as it meant they could no longer ignore or deflect issues. But as a leader, I believe it is our duty to support our subordinates, listen to their concerns, and ensure that problems are being addressed.

The EAC also required each representative to bring forward three possible solutions to the problems they identified. This not only empowered the employees to think critically and proactively about resolving issues but also encouraged ownership of the process. I committed to providing a response within 30 days, ensuring that their voices were heard and actions were taken.

Incorporating this approach into any organization—whether in law enforcement or a corporate setting—can significantly improve morale, trust, and transparency. When employees feel they have a direct line to leadership and know their concerns will be taken seriously, they become more engaged, motivated, and invested in the organization's success. Moreover, this level of transparency cultivates a culture of accountability, where issues are addressed before they escalate and leaders are viewed as responsive and attuned to the needs of their team.

Building Trust Through Vulnerability

Leadership also requires vulnerability. To gain trust, you must give trust. This can feel risky, especially when past experiences with difficult employees have made you cautious. However, if you don't trust your team, it's impossible to build a strong, cohesive unit. I learned this through my own experiences—despite setbacks with some employees, I continued to give trust to those who earned it.

In both law enforcement and the corporate world, trusting your team allows them to step up and take ownership of their roles. Don't let negative experiences with a few individuals make you jaded or reluctant to trust the next person. When you show faith in others, they are more likely to rise to the occasion and take pride in their contributions.

Leading With Purpose

Ultimately, building and leading effective teams is about creating a culture where everyone is committed to a common purpose, where trust and communication are the norms, and where accountability and empowerment drive continuous growth. Whether you're leading a police department, a business, or any other group, these principles are universal. They are the keys to unlocking the full potential of your team and achieving success together.

As you lead your own teams, remember that your role is not just to direct but to inspire, support, and guide. The most successful teams are those that operate as a unit, where every member feels like they belong and where every voice is heard. This is the kind of team that can overcome any challenge, rise to any occasion, and achieve greatness. Whether in law enforcement or corporate environments, these leadership principles will serve you and your team well.

CHAPTER 5 : BUILDING AND LEADING EFFECTIVE TEAMS

Reflect and Apply: Team success is a reflection of leadership. As you wrap up this chapter, consider how you can strengthen your team's trust, communication, and accountability. Head to the **Appendix - Leadership Workbook and Action Plans** to document your strategies for building high-performing teams and empowering your people to achieve their potential.

CHAPTER 6:

COMMUNITY-CENTERED LEADERSHIP

Leadership isn't just about managing a team or achieving organizational goals; it's about understanding and serving the community you're part of. Throughout my career, I've learned that effective leadership in law enforcement—or any field—requires a deep commitment to the people you serve. Building trust, fostering relationships, and engaging with the community are not just strategies; they are essential components of successful leadership.

When I became Chief of Police in Simpsonville, I quickly realized that the department's relationship with the community was strained. Crime rates were high, and there was a significant disconnect between the police and the citizens they were sworn to protect. To address this, I knew we needed to shift our focus from merely enforcing the law to actively building relationships with the community. This meant implementing a community-centered approach to policing, which would later become one of the cornerstones of our success.

Engaging Directly with the Community

One of the first steps I took was to engage directly with community leaders and residents. I attended neighborhood meetings, visited local businesses, and made it a point to be visible and accessible to the public. This wasn't just about being seen; it was about listening to the concerns and needs of the community and demonstrating that the police department was there to serve them. These efforts were instrumental in rebuilding trust and opening lines of communication that had long been closed.

In addition to building relationships through face-to-face engagement, we implemented a series of community-based programs designed to address specific issues within the city. For example, we launched youth outreach initiatives to keep young people on the right path and out of trouble. These initiatives were carried out in partnership with local schools, churches, and civic organizations to create mentorship, education, and positive activities for at-risk youth. Such programs didn't just reduce crime—they helped to build a stronger, more cohesive community where citizens felt supported by law enforcement.

I also believe that living in the community I served was crucial to staying connected and deeply involved. Throughout my career as a two-time Chief of Police, I made it a point to move into the city limits of the jurisdiction I was responsible for. This allowed me to experience the community firsthand—the good and the bad—and be affected by local issues just like every other resident. Chiefs who live outside their jurisdiction often drive into work and back home with their blinders on, removed from the daily realities that affect the people they serve. This can create a perception that they are out of touch or not fully committed.

Living within the community gave me a greater sense of empathy and a stronger commitment to resolving local issues. It wasn't just about policy; it was personal. For example, in one neighborhood where crime rates were particularly high, I experienced those same concerns for my own family's safety, driving me to work even harder to improve public safety. By living in the community, I felt more accountable to the people I served and was even driven by the desire to increase property values, including my own.

In fact, I believe it should be mandatory for chiefs of police to reside in the city limits they serve, as it demonstrates a commitment beyond just holding a title. However, adequate compensation must accompany this requirement to make it feasible, ensuring that those who lead the city can also afford to live within it.

Our collective efforts, from direct engagement to community programs and residency, weren't just about reducing crime—they were about fostering a deeper connection between the police department and the people we served. By embedding ourselves into the community, we were able to identify the issues that mattered most and work collaboratively to address them.

Cancer Awareness Initiative

Another initiative we implemented aimed at community connection and awareness was the creation of a cancer awareness program. As of the writing of this book, the American Cancer Society (ACS) states that more than 40 percent of individuals will be diagnosed with cancer during their lifetime. Cancer has deeply affected so many of us, claiming the lives of loved ones, and we felt it was crucial to address this in a way that could touch many hearts. My staff and I developed the concept of designing and deploying cancer-themed police cars in both agencies where I served as Chief. These specially designed cars were funded through community donations and aimed to spread awareness, spark conversations, and demonstrate our department's deep concern for the well-being of the people we served. It wasn't just about patrolling the streets; it was about showing the community that we cared on a much deeper level, beyond just crime prevention.

In much the same way, businesses that want to become a staple in their communities can adopt a similar approach. A business that engages directly with the community by attending local events, supporting causes that align with community values, and offering accessible services or sponsorships will foster goodwill. This creates a reciprocal relationship where the business gives back to the community, and in turn, the community supports the business. For example, a small business could sponsor local youth sports teams, or larger corporations might fund community improvement projects or offer internships to local students.

Transparency and Building Trust

Another key aspect of community-centered leadership is transparency. In law enforcement, transparency is crucial for building and maintaining public trust. I made it a priority to ensure that the department operated with complete transparency, particularly in our interactions with the community. We established regular communication channels, including public forums and social media, where citizens could ask questions, voice concerns, and receive updates on the department's activities. This openness helped to dispel rumors, reduce fear, and foster a sense of partnership between the police and the community.

Transparency is equally vital in the corporate world. Companies that operate transparently—sharing information on their financial health, social responsibility efforts, and business decisions—earn the trust and loyalty of their customers. Just as I used public forums in law enforcement, businesses can host community events, Q&A sessions, or even virtual town halls where they openly discuss their goals, challenges, and contributions to the local economy. By being transparent, businesses not only foster trust but also show that they are invested in the community's well-being.

Tailoring Leadership to Diverse Communities

In Laurens, I faced a different set of challenges but applied the same community-centered principles. The city had a diverse population with unique needs and concerns. To effectively serve Laurens as Chief of Police, I had to understand the cultural dynamics at play and tailor our approach accordingly. This meant not only addressing crime but also promoting equality and inclusivity within the department and the community. We worked to strengthen relationships with minority communities, ensuring that everyone in Laurens felt safe, valued, and respected.

In the corporate world, it's essential for leaders to recognize and respond to the diverse needs of their customers and employees. Businesses that embrace inclusivity, celebrate diversity, and engage with minority communities will not only foster goodwill but also create a more loyal customer base. This can include offering products or services that cater to different cultural needs, supporting minority-owned businesses, or creating inclusive work environments where all employees feel valued. For small businesses, this could be as simple as hosting cultural events or supporting local minority initiatives, further embedding the business into the fabric of the community.

The Power of Reciprocity in Community-Centered Leadership

One of the most rewarding aspects of community-centered leadership is seeing the tangible impact it has on the lives of the people you serve. In Simpsonville, our efforts led to a 287% increase in drug/narcotics investigations and a significant reduction in crime, ultimately making it the safest city in South Carolina. In Laurens, we made strides in improving public safety and community relations, setting the stage for a brighter future for the city.

This tit-for-tat relationship—where the community supports an organization or business in return for its contributions—is at the heart of community-centered leadership. If a business gives back to the community, the community will support that business, whether through loyalty, word of mouth, or recommendations. This reciprocal relationship strengthens both the organization and the community, creating a positive feedback loop of mutual support.

Leadership as a Service

Community-centered leadership isn't just a strategy; it's a philosophy. It's about recognizing that as leaders, our primary responsibility is to serve the people. This means being responsive to their needs, engaging with them authentically, and working tirelessly to create a safer, more just society. Whether you're leading a police department, a business, or any other organization, the principles of community-centered leadership are universal. They remind us that leadership is not about power or control—it's about service, compassion, and making a positive impact on the world around us.

In corporate America and small businesses, leaders must embrace the same philosophy of service-oriented leadership. This involves understanding the needs of both the community and the customer base, creating solutions that address those needs, and making the community a partner in the business's success. Businesses that serve their communities, rather than merely extracting value from them, become staples in those communities, ensuring long-term sustainability and loyalty.

Conclusion: A Universal Approach to Leadership

As you continue on your leadership journey, I encourage you to embrace these principles. Build relationships, foster trust, and always keep the needs of the community at the forefront of your decisions. In doing so, you'll not only achieve success but also make a lasting difference in the lives of those you lead. Whether you are leading a team of police officers, employees in a corporate setting, or a small business, the principles of community-centered leadership are universal—and they will guide you to success and a meaningful, lasting impact on your community.

CHAPTER 6 : COMMUNITY-CENTERED LEADERSHIP

Reflect and Apply: A community-centered approach to leadership fosters trust and partnership. Reflect on how you can better engage with the communities you serve. Turn to the **Appendix - Leadership Workbook and Action Plans** to document your plans for building relationships, fostering inclusivity, and driving positive change through community-focused leadership.

CHAPTER 7:

THE ABILITY TO MAKE DECISIONS

As a leader, the ability to make decisions quickly and effectively is crucial. When you're at the top, procrastination can be detrimental. While some decisions require careful thought, others need to be made swiftly to keep the organization moving forward. Indecisiveness is one of the most frustrating traits a leader can exhibit, and it can erode the confidence your team has in your leadership. Whether in law enforcement or the private sector, decision-making is the core of leadership that drives an organization towards success.

I. The Importance of Decisiveness

Indecisiveness can paralyze an organization. Teams look to their leaders for direction, especially in challenging situations. As a leader, you must be able to assess the situation, weigh your options, and make a decision. Over my 26 years of law enforcement, one of the biggest issues I have seen is personnel viewing their bosses as weak or incompetent because of their inability or fear to make decisions without asking for permission. If the top cop cannot make a decision without asking their boss (such as a city administrator or city manager), they are not effective leaders. Leadership demands the confidence to make decisions independently, especially on day-to-day matters. Leaders cannot fear mistakes in small daily activities. However, if a major decision arises, it is often wise to consult with others to ensure the best course of action.

In corporate environments or small businesses, decisiveness helps maintain momentum. An indecisive leader creates a ripple effect of confusion, causing projects to stall and reducing team morale. Customers and clients expect timely decisions, whether related to products, services, or partnerships. Strong leaders in the business world are known for their ability to make informed decisions quickly, which ultimately positions their companies ahead of competitors.

II. Owning Mistakes and Driving Change

Making decisions also means accepting the responsibility that comes with them. Not every decision will be the right one, but the willingness to own mistakes and correct course is a mark of true leadership. One of the most common signs of poor leadership is the tendency to blame others for one's own incompetencies. When a leader fails to take responsibility for the actions and decisions of their team, it demonstrates a lack of accountability. Every decision or action within an organization is the leader's responsibility. Whether good or bad, own it, learn from it, and move on. If a mistake is made, it is important to communicate to the public and stakeholders how the mistake will be corrected, including the measures put in place to prevent a recurrence, such as enhanced training or procedural changes. Leaders who fail to take ownership create a culture of deflection and defensiveness, which ultimately erodes trust.

In law enforcement, owning mistakes is essential to maintaining trust with the community and your team. For example, in decisions related to strategy, personnel, or operations, accountability is key. When I made decisions that didn't yield the expected results, I was transparent about them. This honesty helped build a culture of accountability, where my team understood that mistakes could be opportunities for learning, not excuses for inaction.

In the corporate sector, leaders must embrace failure as part of growth. Businesses that innovate and take risks often face setbacks, but the ability to pivot and adjust quickly is what separates successful companies from stagnant ones. Leaders who take responsibility for their choices—both good and bad—instill a culture of innovation and resilience.

III. Impact of Leadership on Organizational Culture

The culture of an organization is often a reflection of its leadership. As a leader, your ability to make decisions—both big and small—sets the tone for how your team operates. When employees see that their leader is decisive and takes responsibility for outcomes, they are more likely to adopt a proactive and accountable approach themselves. Conversely, a leader who hesitates or avoids making tough calls can create a culture of uncertainty and passivity.

In law enforcement, when officers see that leadership is committed to making tough decisions, whether it's about holding officers accountable or adapting policies for community relations, it creates a proactive culture of responsibility. Officers are encouraged to make their own decisions in the field, knowing that leadership supports timely and necessary action.

Similarly, in business, the decisions made by leaders shape organizational culture. Leaders who are decisive and transparent foster a work environment where employees feel empowered to take ownership of their roles and contribute ideas. A culture of decisiveness breeds innovation, encourages initiative, and builds confidence across all levels of the organization.

IV. Handling Opposition

Leaders who are agents of change will inevitably face opposition. If you remain in a leadership role for an extended period and never encounter resistance, it's likely that you are not pushing the organization forward. It is essential to understand that if you do not have opposition, you are not doing anything meaningful. A leader who stays in their role for years and is considered a "nice guy" but never faces criticism likely avoids taking a stance on issues of great importance. Effective leadership means making tough decisions that won't always be popular but are necessary for growth and progress.

If people are talking about you, it's a sign you are making progress. People do not waste time discussing individuals who do nothing. However, they often talk negatively about great leaders who bring about change—sometimes out of jealousy, resistance to change, or discomfort. Staying the course through opposition is vital to achieving success. Consistency and resilience are how leaders achieve greatness. For instance, when I led change in departments, many resisted at first, but ultimately, the results spoke for themselves. My steadfastness in the face of opposition led to significant improvements, which earned the respect of those who initially doubted the direction. In corporate America and small businesses, leaders often face pushback when implementing new strategies or changes. Whether it's restructuring, adopting new technologies, or launching new initiatives, resistance is inevitable. However, leaders who stay focused on long-term goals and communicate the vision clearly can guide their teams through periods of discomfort, ultimately driving the company forward.

V. Decision-Making in Leadership: A Common Principle in Law Enforcement and Business

While decision-making is critical in both law enforcement and business, the principle is universal. Whether you're deciding on the next operational move in a police department or choosing a market expansion strategy for a company, the fundamentals remain the same. Leaders must:

- **Assess the Situation**: Gather the facts, understand the environment, and consider potential risks and rewards.
- **Make Timely Decisions**: Delaying decisions can harm both the organization and its stakeholders. A decision, even if imperfect, often propels the organization forward.
- **Own the Outcome**: Whether the decision leads to success or failure, take full responsibility. This builds credibility and trust with your team and stakeholders.
- **Handle Resistance with Confidence**: Change often comes with opposition. Stay focused on the end goal, communicate clearly, and remain open to feedback while driving progress.

In both law enforcement and business, the ability to make decisions defines the leader's effectiveness. In law enforcement, it can mean the difference between a proactive, engaged department and one that is reactionary. In business, timely decisions can determine whether a company thrives in a competitive market or falls behind.

Conclusion

The ability to make decisions is a critical aspect of leadership. It involves assessing situations, making timely decisions, owning mistakes, and driving change. The effectiveness of your decisions directly impacts the culture and success of your organization. Whether you're in law enforcement or leading a business, decisive leadership is essential to moving your team forward. As a leader, you must be willing to take risks, make difficult choices, and navigate the challenges that come with leadership. By applying these principles in both public service and the private sector, you can foster a culture of accountability, adaptability, and success.

CHAPTER 7 : THE ABILITY TO MAKE DECISIONS

Reflect and Apply: Decisiveness is a core element of leadership. Reflect on your decision-making process and how it affects your team and organization. To refine your approach, use the **Appendix - Leadership Workbook and Action Plans** to document your decision-making principles, assess your recent decisions, and identify ways to improve.

CHAPTER 8:

PROGRESSIVE DISCIPLINE AND ACCOUNTABILITY

As a leader, one of the most challenging responsibilities is disciplining employees. Whether in law enforcement or corporate America, discipline is not just about punishment—it's an opportunity to correct behavior and provide guidance for growth. This chapter covers the importance of progressive discipline, the nuances of accountability, and the hard choices leaders face when individuals refuse to take responsibility for their actions.

Progressive Discipline: A Fair Approach

Progressive discipline is a structured way of guiding employees to improve by addressing behavior issues gradually. It starts with coaching, verbal warnings, written warnings, and performance improvement plans, escalating to more formal actions like suspension or demotion if necessary. This allows employees the opportunity to reflect and correct their actions.

In law enforcement, where public safety is at stake, the balance is particularly delicate. For example, as Chief of Police, I had to implement progressive discipline not just to maintain public trust, but also to give officers a chance to improve while still holding them accountable. However, in situations involving severe violations- especially those that posed significant public safety risks or involved criminal allegations- a more immediate, decisive response was required.

Similarly, in corporate settings, the stakes may not always be life and death, but the same principles apply. For example, if a financial officer repeatedly mismanages accounts, the company's reputation and stability are at risk. Just like in policing, escalating discipline through coaching and performance plans can work, but swift termination may be necessary for egregious violations.

The Fine Line Between Correction and Morale

While discipline is necessary, how it's carried out makes all the difference. As a leader, I've always adhered to the principle of "praise in public, discipline in private." The goal of discipline should always be to preserve dignity while correcting behavior.

For instance, there have been many cases where I had to discipline officers. Most accepted it as a learning opportunity, thanked me afterward, and even grew from the experience. However, not every individual reacts this way. Some resist the correction, refuse accountability, and even lash out.

This reality is not limited to law enforcement. Imagine a top sales executive who consistently misses targets despite multiple interventions. Their peers may watch closely to see how leadership handles the situation, and a public reprimand could cause ripples across the organization, damaging morale. Disciplining this executive in a private, respectful manner, while holding them accountable, sends a message of fairness and professionalism to the team.

The Challenges of Accountability

Accountability is one of the most difficult aspects of leadership. Not everyone is willing to take responsibility for their mistakes, and as a leader, you'll often find that when you push for accountability, resistance emerges.

In my career as Chief of Police, I encountered this with a particularly talented Corporal who repeatedly violated safety protocols. Despite multiple interventions- including mentorship programs and personal guidance—his behavior did not improve. Ultimately, I had to terminate him. Instead of reflecting on his own actions, he used social media to publicly attack me and even tried to blackmail me for a positive recommendation in exchange for removing his negative online reviews of my book series.

This incident taught me a key leadership lesson: you can't always control how people will respond to accountability, but you must stand firm in holding them responsible.

In corporate America, the same dynamics occur. A senior manager, after being disciplined for repeated HR violations, might respond by spreading negativity about the company or the CEO. Whether in law enforcement or business, leaders must be prepared to face these challenges and maintain their course, knowing that accountability is non-negotiable.

FDD Story: Accountability on a Larger Scale

During my time as the National Supervisor for U.S. police mentors and advisors in Afghanistan, I was responsible for overseeing over 140 U.S. personnel as part of the Focus District Development (FDD) program. Our mission was to rebuild over 50 Afghan police departments from the ground up and create stability around a nationwide trade route essential for Afghanistan's economic future.

The individuals under my command were often deployed to some of the most dangerous regions imaginable, where the threat of death was ever-present. The responsibility of selecting who would go into these hazardous areas weighed heavily on me. Most personnel embraced their duty with professionalism, knowing the risks. However, three individuals chose to blame me for their undesirable assignments rather than take responsibility.

Instead of accepting their deployment, they filed complaints that reached up the chain of command. Unfortunately, leadership above me failed to discipline them, allowing them to avoid deployment altogether. This sent a destructive message to the rest of the team: if you complain enough, you can avoid the hardest assignments. The result was a severe blow to morale and a weakening of accountability across the unit.

This experience reinforced a vital lesson for any leader: accountability must be maintained at every level. When leadership fails to align on this issue, the entire structure can begin to crumble. Whether you're leading a military operation or managing a corporate team, the principles of accountability remain the same.

CHAPTER 8 : PROGRESSIVE DISCIPLINE AND ACCOUNTABILITY

Reflect and Apply: Progressive discipline and accountability are essential components of effective leadership. Reflect on how you approach these tasks within your organization and consider their impact on team morale and organizational culture. To ensure fairness and professionalism, use the **Appendix - Leadership Workbook and Action Plans** to document your strategies for handling these situations, assess recent disciplinary actions, and plan for improvements in your process.

CHAPTER 9:

TERMINATION, LAYOFFS, AND EMPATHETIC LEADERSHIP

While progressive discipline can guide employees toward improvement, there are situations where termination becomes unavoidable. Whether due to performance issues or organizational changes, termination and layoffs require leaders to approach these decisions with compassion, ensuring that they are handled ethically and fairly.

Termination: Balancing Tough Decisions with Humanity

Having been wrongfully terminated myself, I know the deep emotional toll it can take on an individual and their family. This personal experience shaped how I approach terminations. Even when necessary, termination should be carried out with professionalism and respect.

In law enforcement, I had to make many tough decisions when officers became liabilities to public safety. For example, one officer repeatedly violated individuals' constitutional rights, despite numerous opportunities to correct his behavior. His termination, while difficult, was necessary for the safety of the community. However, even in these cases, it was crucial to handle the process with dignity and respect.

The same principles apply in corporate environments. Consider a CFO who repeatedly fails to meet financial targets, putting the company at risk. While termination may be necessary, how it's handled matters. Escorting them out in a public manner or cutting off their access before even discussing the situation only damages the company's culture. A private, professional approach, where the individual's dignity is maintained, sends a much stronger message of leadership integrity.

Layoffs: Compassion in the Face of Business Decisions

Layoffs present a different challenge from terminations because they are often driven by external factors—economic downturns, restructuring, or company financial losses. As a leader, laying off employees is one of the most emotionally charged tasks, but it must be done with empathy.

When I was laid off as Director of Compliance due to financial losses, I experienced firsthand how important it is to approach layoffs with transparency. It's essential to be honest about the reasons behind the decision and provide support to help the individual transition.

One of the most powerful examples in my career was when I had to lay off an officer. Rather than simply handing him the notice, I took the extra step of calling a neighboring police department, providing a reference, and ensuring he had a new job lined up. His gratitude was overwhelming, and it turned a painful layoff into a smooth transition for him and his family. In corporate environments, leaders can do the same by offering severance packages, outplacement services, or even personal recommendations.

Corporate Parallels: Empathy and Dignity in the Boardroom

In both law enforcement and corporate leadership, handling layoffs and terminations with empathy is critical. Consider a CEO who must downsize a department due to budget cuts. Instead of abruptly terminating employees, they can offer transitional services, severance pay, or even personalized assistance in finding new roles. These compassionate gestures not only maintain the company's reputation but also preserve relationships that could be valuable in the future.

In the end, the way leaders handle discipline, termination, and layoffs reflects their values. Whether you're leading a police department or a global corporation, treating people with empathy during their most vulnerable moments leaves a lasting impact.

CHAPTER 9 : TERMINATION, LAYOFFS, AND EMPATHETIC LEADERSHIP

Reflect and Apply: Handling terminations and layoffs with empathy is one of the most difficult aspects of leadership. Reflect on your approach to these critical decisions and how they impact your team and the individuals involved. To ensure fairness and professionalism, use the **Appendix - Leadership Workbook and Action Plans** to document your strategies for handling these situations, assess recent terminations or layoffs, and plan for improvements in your process.

CHAPTER 10:

WHY PEOPLE DON'T QUIT JOBS, THEY QUIT LEADERS

POLICE LINE DO NOT CROSS POLICE LINE DO NOT CROSS POLICE LINE DO NOT CROSS

Leadership plays a powerful role in employee retention. People often leave organizations not because of the job itself but because of leadership—or the lack thereof. A leader's ability to create a positive culture, make decisive decisions, and foster a supportive environment is key to keeping talented employees engaged and committed. This principle applies not only in law enforcement but also in corporate America and small businesses, where employee retention can make or break an organization's success.

The Importance of Diverse Leadership Backgrounds

A diverse leadership background is essential for effective decision-making and team management. Leaders who have only worked in one place or one specific environment may not fully understand the broader range of leadership techniques and strategies available to them. Exposure to different environments and challenges equips a leader with the ability to handle varied and unexpected situations.

For example, when I became Chief of Police in Simpsonville and Laurens, my wide range of experiences from different departments and environments helped me address the unique challenges of each department. Whether I was dealing with under-staffing, low morale, or specific crime-related issues, my diverse background gave me the flexibility to implement strategies that worked.

A key element of gaining this broad leadership experience is networking. Networking allows leaders to collaborate with others in the field who have faced similar challenges. By learning from the experiences—and even mistakes—of others, leaders can avoid potential pitfalls and make more informed decisions. Furthermore, networking can help you identify mentors who can offer guidance and support as you navigate complex leadership roles.

However, diverse leadership experience can sometimes be intimidating to those who have spent their entire careers in one place or setting. Individuals who lack exposure to different environments may feel threatened by a leader who brings new perspectives. Before introducing significant changes, it's important to show team members or peers that you genuinely care about them and their contributions. Building trust through personal connections can alleviate feelings of insecurity and resistance. This approach allows leaders to gradually introduce new strategies and win over those who may initially feel uncomfortable with new ideas.

In business, this principle is equally important. Leaders who have worked in different industries or roles are more likely to bring fresh perspectives and innovative solutions to their teams. However, in organizations where individuals have spent years working under a single type of leadership, new ideas can be met with resistance. A tactful leader builds rapport and demonstrates genuine investment in their team before introducing new strategies, fostering collaboration and reducing potential friction.

Retention and Leadership Turnover

Leadership turnover can have a profound impact on an organization, whether in law enforcement or corporate settings. When a well-respected leader departs, it often triggers resignations from employees who were committed to that leader's vision. This is particularly true when relationships and trust have been built over time. In both sectors, a leader's departure can create a ripple effect, undermining the stability and direction of the organization.

The average tenure for a Chief of Police has decreased, now averaging about two years, which is significantly shorter than in the past when chiefs held their positions for much longer. Several factors contribute to this decline in tenure, reflecting the evolving demands of leadership in policing and the heightened expectations placed on chiefs today.

A major factor is the rise of public accountability. In years past, police chiefs operated with less scrutiny from the general public. Today, however, thanks to the influence of social media and constant news coverage, every decision made by a law enforcement leader is subject to intense public examination. The demand for transparency has created a higher level of accountability, but it also places chiefs under enormous pressure. Even minor incidents can be magnified through the lens of social media, where public opinion forms rapidly, often before all facts are known. Chiefs are judged not only by their superiors but also by the broader community, which makes the position increasingly precarious.

Expectations for police chiefs have also risen significantly. Today's chiefs are expected to be much more than operational leaders; they must also be public figures adept at managing community relations, navigating complex political landscapes, and maintaining transparency. These expectations demand that chiefs balance confidentiality, legal concerns, and public relations, all while responding to a more vocal and engaged public. As transparency grows, the public's ability to scrutinize leadership is more immediate and unforgiving, and if a chief fails to meet these heightened expectations, public confidence can erode quickly.

Social media has further amplified the voice of the community, accelerating the spread of both praise and criticism. In an era where a viral post or video can spark nationwide attention, police chiefs are under constant pressure to respond to crises quickly and effectively. This immediate scrutiny can make it difficult to focus on long-term strategies, as short-term controversies and public relations issues often take precedence. As a result, the position has become far more volatile, contributing to shorter tenures.

Another factor contributing to shorter leadership terms is the growing complexity of modern law enforcement issues. Chiefs today must navigate a wide range of social issues, such as police reform, community policing initiatives, use of force debates, and diversity within the ranks. These issues are often politically charged, requiring chiefs to balance community needs with operational effectiveness. The increased demand for reforms in policing has further complicated the role, making it more difficult for chiefs to maintain their positions over time.

Internally, chiefs are also facing more vocal opposition from within their own ranks. Officers and staff, who may resist reforms or new policies, can create friction, making the role even more challenging. This internal resistance, combined with external pressures, has made the position of Chief of Police more difficult to sustain over the long term.

In my own experience, after I left Laurens, over 35% of the staff resigned within six months—people who had believed in the long-term goals we had set for the department. These individuals were committed to the vision I had for the department, and their departure underscores the critical link between leadership and retention. Strong leadership fosters loyalty, while instability at the top can lead to employee turnover and organizational disruption.

In corporate America, leadership turnover has a similar effect. When a respected leader departs, employees may begin to question the company's direction and their own place within it. High turnover among senior management often leads to uncertainty, with employees doubting the long-term vision of the company. This disruption to the organizational culture can impact morale and, ultimately, reduce overall performance. Just as in law enforcement, leadership stability is crucial for maintaining employee loyalty and ensuring organizational continuity.

Whether in law enforcement or business, the departure of key leaders can lead to a period of uncertainty, where employees feel unmoored and unsure of their future within the organization. Leadership turnover, especially at senior levels, must be managed carefully to prevent an exodus of talent and a loss of the trust that has been carefully built over time.

By understanding the modern pressures of leadership turnover- whether due to public accountability, internal challenges, or rising expectations- organizations can better prepare for leadership transitions and minimize the negative impacts on morale and performance.

Creating a Culture That Retains Talent

A leader's primary responsibility is to create a culture where employees feel valued, supported, and motivated to perform at their best. In both police departments I led, I inherited agencies with significant understaffing issues. Through focused leadership and a commitment to building a positive culture, we achieved 100% staffing in two separate agencies, despite surrounding agencies struggling to fill positions. This success came from fostering a culture of inclusivity, recognition, and accountability that attracted top talent.

What made this even more remarkable was that we were able to hire certified officers willing to leave larger agencies and take positions in a smaller department, even for less money and lower rank. These individuals wanted to be part of something they believed in—something bigger than just a job. They saw leadership they trusted, a clear mission, and a supportive environment, and were willing to make sacrifices to join. This speaks to the power of creating a strong organizational culture—one that not only retains talent but draws in highly qualified individuals.

Another key to retaining talent is ensuring that employees know their leadership has their back, especially when they face public scrutiny. As a Chief, you have to be willing to sacrifice your own reputation to support your team when necessary. If employees know you will stand by them, they will give their best effort. But if they doubt your support, they will hesitate, fearing one bad-looking moment could cost them their career.

Recognizing employee successes, offering opportunities for professional growth, and addressing challenges transparently are also key components of building a positive work environment. In business, creating a culture of trust and opportunity can foster loyalty. When employees feel their contributions are valued and they are given the tools to grow, they are far more likely to stay.

The Ability to Make Decisions

Decisiveness is a fundamental quality of strong leadership. Whether in law enforcement or business, hesitation can lead to missed opportunities. What sets great leaders apart is their willingness to own mistakes and course-correct when needed.

One of the most rewarding aspects of leadership is seeing cultural shifts in organizations. Employees often thanked me for holding others accountable, especially those who had previously evaded responsibility. Accountability is critical in driving an organization forward and ensuring that all members of the team are held to the same high standards.

Finding the Right Fit

Not every employee will be the right fit for every leader or organization. Throughout my tenure as a Chief of Police, I made difficult decisions about individuals who weren't the right fit for the agency's direction. One of the toughest lessons I learned was the importance of getting rid of toxic employees quickly. Toxic employees undermine morale, productivity, and the cohesiveness of the team.

Even if staffing numbers are low, it's critical to remove toxic individuals as soon as you recognize the damage they cause. In the long run, it's better to operate with a smaller, more cohesive team than to let a toxic presence degrade the organization from within.

In corporate America, leaders face similar challenges. Recognizing when someone doesn't fit the team dynamic or organizational vision is critical for maintaining a positive work environment. Great leaders guide employees toward roles that better suit their skills—even if that means helping them transition out of the organization.

The Role of Leadership in Retention, with a Focus on Officer Wellness

Retention hinges on the leadership environment you create. Employees need to feel that their leader genuinely cares about them, values their contributions, and supports their growth. Over the years, I implemented several initiatives to address the holistic well-being of officers in the agencies I led.

These included a Peer Support Team, an in-house gym, a therapy dog program, and a Police Chaplain Program. We also established a Wives Club to support the families of officers and launched an annual

Christmas float for officers and their families. These initiatives reinforced that we were more than just a department—we were a family.

Supporting Employee Well-Being through Leadership

Supporting employee well-being involves promoting work-life balance, mental health, and physical health. Flexible scheduling, avoiding over-reliance on overtime, and making sure employees use vacation time all help prevent burnout.

We introduced peer support groups and counseling services to address mental health needs, particularly for those struggling with PTSD or other trauma-related conditions. Physical health initiatives included the installation of a gym and partnerships with the YMCA for free family memberships. These efforts improved morale, camaraderie, and overall well-being.

Conclusion

People don't quit jobs—they quit leaders. A leader's ability to create a culture of support, trust, and accountability, while prioritizing the well-being of their employees, can significantly impact retention. When leaders invest in their team's holistic health, they foster an engaged, motivated, and loyal workforce. By building a positive, inclusive, and empowering environment, leaders can ensure that their team remains committed and driven, even through challenges.

CHAPTER 10 : WHY PEOPLE DON'T QUIT JOBS, THEY QUIT LEADERS

Reflect and Apply: Leadership plays a crucial role in retention. Consider how your leadership style impacts your team's motivation and loyalty. Use the **Appendix - Leadership Workbook and Action Plans** to assess your leadership impact, identify areas for improvement, and set goals for creating a culture that encourages retention and long-term commitment.

CHAPTER 11:

THE ART OF DELEGATION AND EMPOWERMENT

As a new leader, I was determined to prove myself by taking on as much responsibility as possible. I wanted to be involved in every decision and ensure everything was done perfectly. This approach quickly led to working 90-plus hour weeks, leaving me exhausted and struggling to keep up. I thought I was being an effective leader by handling everything myself, but in reality, I was burning out and stifling the potential of my team.

It wasn't long before I realized that this approach was unsustainable. Not only was I overworked, but my team was also underutilized and disengaged. They were looking to me for direction, but I wasn't giving them the opportunity to take ownership of their work. This was a turning point in my leadership journey—I needed to learn the art of delegation.

The Struggle with Letting Go

Delegation was difficult at first. Like many new leaders, I was hesitant to let go of control. I worried that if I didn't oversee every aspect of a project, something would go wrong. But as I began to delegate tasks to my team, I noticed something surprising: not only were things not falling apart, but they were actually getting done more efficiently. My team members were stepping up, taking ownership of their tasks, and producing excellent results, all while I was still providing oversight and steering them toward our goals if needed.

Delegating allowed me to focus on the bigger picture—on strategy and vision—while trusting my team to handle the details. This shift didn't happen overnight, and it required me to build trust in my team's abilities. But as I did, we accomplished more with less effort. My work weeks became more manageable, and I no longer carried the weight of every task on my own.

The Pitfalls of Micromanagement and the Power of Trust

I learned early on that micromanagement is not a sustainable way to lead. People in leadership positions who fall into the trap of micromanagement are often driven by fear—fear of losing control or fear of being exposed as incompetent. These leaders answer their fears by tightening their grip on every detail, spying on their people, creating unreasonable policies, and even driving away talented individuals who might pose a threat to their fragile sense of authority. This kind of leadership is toxic. It turns into a cycle of mistrust, control, and paranoia, eroding the team's morale and leading to long-term dysfunction.

My former staff members witnessed the consequences of this type of leadership firsthand after I left one of the agencies where I had served as Chief of Police. The next person who took over immediately began micromanaging everything—from office supply spending down to the dollar, to how many copies people could make on the printer. What started as financial oversight soon escalated into deeper insecurity and paranoia. This Chief even resorted to sneaking into his subordinates' offices after hours, fearful that they might have information that could undermine him.

It all came to light when one of his command staff members, suspecting someone was tampering with their office, set up a hidden camera. To everyone's surprise, it was the Chief himself caught going through locked drawers and personal items. This discovery caused a massive loss of trust within the department, resulting in a more than 25% staff exodus. The damage to his legacy as a leader was irreparable. This is an extreme example of how fear-driven micromanagement can spiral out of control and lead to unethical behavior. Leaders who act out of fear, trying to protect a position they're not ready or qualified for, will inevitably create environments where trust and growth are impossible.

True leaders, on the other hand, surround themselves with people who are smarter and more skilled than they are. They don't fear their team's competence—they embrace it. These leaders encourage their team members to grow, give them the freedom to excel, and build them up at every opportunity. By empowering others, they create an organization that thrives because everyone is contributing at their highest level. This is how greatness is achieved—not through control, but through trust, delegation, and empowerment.

Empowering the Team

Delegation isn't just about handing off tasks; it's about empowering your team to take ownership of their work. When you delegate effectively, you give your team members the authority and responsibility to make decisions, solve problems, and take initiative. This empowerment leads to greater buy-in and accountability. Team members feel valued and trusted, which boosts their motivation and commitment to the success of the project.

In law enforcement, I saw this firsthand when I trusted officers to take the lead on investigations or community programs. Not only did they complete their tasks—they excelled. They took pride in their work, knowing they contributed to the department's success. When things didn't go as planned, they were more willing to take responsibility and learn because they had ownership of the outcomes.

It's important to recognize that mistakes will be made along the way. What matters is the intent behind the mistake—did the team member have good intentions, or was there negligence? If they made an honest mistake while trying to do their best, it's a coaching opportunity. Leaders need to foster an environment where failure is seen as a chance to learn. This builds a culture where team members think outside the box and innovate without fear of punishment.

Putting Your Best Foot Forward in Leadership

While learning the art of delegation allows a leader to focus on high-level strategic initiatives, it's important to remember that this shift also frees up time to embody leadership values that set the tone for the organization. Delegation isn't about doing less, it's about doing more where it matters most—at the leadership level. This is where you can focus on high-impact decisions, strategic thinking, and demonstrating the core values of leadership that inspire those around you.

As a leader, I've always believed that if you want to be the greatest worker, leader, or partner, you must consistently put your best foot forward. This means giving your greatest effort and working harder than anyone else in the room, regardless of the circumstances. Great leaders have a habit of exceeding expectations, making them invaluable team members and a solid investment for any organization. In contrast, average individuals often avoid doing more than what's required, citing that they aren't being paid extra for it. However, it's important not to focus on what you aren't being compensated for now- doing your best will pay off later when you're rewarded with top-tier leadership opportunities. This internal drive for excellence is what sets strong leaders apart. It's not just about completing tasks; it's about demonstrating the commitment and work ethic that will inspire others to follow your example.

I remember, as Chief of Police in Laurens, when we had to temporarily move out of our police department into a much smaller space for a year while the old department underwent major renovations. Moving an entire police force is challenging under any circumstances, but being forced to relocate into a building that wasn't ready to occupy was a completely different hurdle. The city had sold the previous building, and with the project already six months behind schedule, we had no choice but to move into the unfinished site or risk having nowhere to call home. This was also the second move our department had undergone in one year- a huge stressor for any new Chief of Police. We had to adapt quickly to working in a construction zone. The noise, dust, power failures, equipment not fully installed, and limited workspace made it a difficult environment, and as the leader, I knew my team needed more than just orders—they needed to see that I was willing to get my hands dirty alongside them.

I spent countless hours doing non-police work to ensure the officers had the most comfortable environment possible. From mopping the floors twice a day to keep the dust down to working on the weekends to keep things clean, I did whatever it took to make things more manageable. I even made sure their patrol room was set up first, so they could focus on their duties. This wasn't something I mandated—it was something I did because of my commitment to servant leadership.

And the effect was contagious. Soon, a group of officers began to follow my lead, stepping up and volunteering to do the same. We took pride in doing whatever was needed, whether it was cleaning bathrooms, wet-vacuuming leaks in the middle of the night, or landscaping around the station. It became clear to me that when you set an example of putting your best foot forward, it creates a ripple effect. My willingness to go beyond what was expected fostered a culture of teamwork, pride, and mutual respect. It wasn't about rank or title—it was about shared responsibility and pride in our work environment.

This mindset ties directly into the concept of effective delegation. By empowering your team to take ownership of their roles, you create space for yourself to focus on these high-level tasks. But never lose sight of the fact that leadership is not just about strategy; it's about showing up in ways that matter. The willingness to work harder than anyone else in the room sets the tone for the kind of commitment you want from your team. Demonstrating servant leadership- where no job is too small- fosters loyalty and inspires others to follow suit.

In conclusion, delegation isn't about doing less—it's about doing more where it counts. As you delegate tasks and empower your team, take the opportunity to step into higher-level roles that can inspire and motivate. Lead by example, put your best foot forward, and show your team that there is no task beneath you. Whether it's making strategic decisions or simply mopping the floor to create a better workspace, it's this level of commitment and work ethic that will create a culture of dedication and teamwork, allowing your organization to thrive.

This principle of servant leadership- of doing what is needed to support your team—reflects the importance of fostering an environment where everyone feels empowered to contribute. When you never settle and always give your best effort, your team will do the same, and together, you can accomplish far more than you ever could alone.

Avoiding the Pitfall of Overworking Your Best People

One of the biggest challenges of delegation is ensuring that you don't overburden your most dependable team members. It's tempting to lean on them for every important task because they always deliver, but overworking them can lead to burnout and resentment. It's crucial to distribute work evenly across the team, giving everyone a chance to grow.

This can be difficult when some team members require more guidance. However, by identifying potential in less-experienced individuals and delegating tasks to them, you can develop their capabilities and prevent burnout among your top performers. Sometimes, those you least expect will step up and excel when they find a project that ignites their passion.

At the same time, it's important to hold underperformers accountable. Allowing slackers to get away with doing little can demoralize the rest of the team. Make sure everyone understands their responsibilities and knows there are consequences for not meeting expectations.

The Importance of Rewarding and Promoting Talent

Recognizing and rewarding those who excel is a critical part of effective delegation. When you delegate tasks and people rise to the occasion, their hard work should not go unnoticed. As a leader, it's important to publicly acknowledge their contributions and reward them with opportunities for further growth, such as promotions.

In law enforcement leadership, this is particularly important. Let's say you have an officer who consistently goes above and beyond—perhaps they lead community outreach programs or consistently solve high-profile cases. Rewarding them with a promotion is a way to show that their hard work is valued. However, leaders sometimes fall into the trap of not promoting top performers out of fear of losing their "workhorse." While it's tempting to keep your best people in the roles they excel at, it's unfair to hold them back from advancing their careers. If an individual has earned a promotion and desires it, it's important to support their growth, even if it means they'll be in a different role.

For example, as Chief of Police, I had an officer who was exceptional at organizing and managing community events. When a Lieutenant position became available, I knew he deserved it. Although it meant I'd be losing his talents in the community relations role, he earned the promotion. By supporting his career advancement, not only did he become a better leader, but he also continued to mentor others. Promoting people who deserve it sends a clear message to the entire organization that hard work and talent are rewarded, which helps build morale and motivation throughout the team.

The Benefits of Delegation

The benefits of delegation go beyond lightening your workload. It creates a culture of collaboration, innovation, and continuous improvement. When team members are empowered to make decisions and take action, they bring diverse perspectives and ideas to the table, leading to more creative solutions. In fact, as a leader, you can accomplish far more by working together as a team than you could ever achieve on your own. By tapping into the collective strengths, knowledge, and talents of your team, you leverage the power of collaboration to achieve results that would be impossible for a single person to deliver.

Additionally, delegation helps develop future leaders by giving your team the chance to take on new challenges and grow in their roles. This builds leadership potential within the organization, ensuring a strong pipeline of capable individuals ready to step up when needed. A team that operates cohesively can cover more ground, spot potential pitfalls faster, and generate a wider array of solutions than an individual leader managing everything on their own. The combined efforts of a well-delegated team can tackle complex challenges more effectively, as each member contributes their unique strengths and expertise.

For example, I once delegated a critical aspect of a task force operation to a junior officer who had never handled such responsibilities before. I provided oversight but trusted him to lead. Not only did the operation go smoothly, but this officer's confidence grew immensely. Within a year, he was leading similar operations independently, which showed me the power of delegation in leadership development. When you delegate, you not only amplify your own leadership impact but also create an environment where the team achieves more than the sum of its parts.

How to Delegate Effectively

Effective delegation requires clear communication and trust. Here are key steps for successful delegation:

- **Identify the Right Tasks to Delegate**: Not all tasks should be delegated. Delegate tasks that are within your team's capabilities or that will help them grow.
- **Choose the Right People**: Match tasks with team members based on their strengths and interests. This increases the likelihood of success and engagement.
- **Provide Clear Instructions**: Communicate desired outcomes, deadlines, and any necessary guidelines. Avoid micromanaging—allow your team to approach tasks their own way. Periodic updates will ensure things stay on track.
- **Offer Support**: Let your team know that you're available for guidance if needed, but give them the space to own the task. Encourage them to lean on peers for support.
- **Trust the Process**: Trust that your team will deliver. Use mistakes as learning opportunities rather than reasons to take back control.
- **Recognize and Reward**: Acknowledge your team's efforts and successes. Recognition reinforces their contributions and fosters a sense of ownership.

The Impact of Delegation on Leadership

Learning to delegate not only transformed my leadership style but also enhanced my team's effectiveness. I could focus on long-term goals and strategic initiatives, while the team handled the day-to-day operations. This shift increased productivity, boosted morale, and created a more engaged workforce. It also allowed me to maintain focus on larger issues, rather than getting bogged down in minor details.

In law enforcement, delegation can make the difference between a stagnant department and one that innovates and excels. Empowering your team fosters a sense of ownership and collaboration, and creates a work environment where leadership is shared, success is collective, and the burden is lighter for everyone.

The art of delegation is not just about getting tasks off your plate; it's about building a culture of trust, empowerment, and shared success. Whether you're leading in law enforcement or any other sector, mastering this skill will help you unlock the potential of your team and lead your organization to greater success.

CHAPTER 11 : THE ART OF DELEGATION AND EMPOWERMENT

Reflect and Apply: Effective delegation empowers your team and lightens your load. Reflect on how you currently delegate tasks and empower others to lead. Head to the **Appendix - Leadership Workbook and Action Plans** to document your delegation strategies and identify opportunities to trust your team with greater responsibility.

CHAPTER 12:

ADAPTING TO CULTURAL CHALLENGES

Leadership today goes beyond managing teams and making decisions; it requires the ability to adapt to a variety of cultural landscapes. This is especially true in law enforcement, where the communities we serve are often composed of diverse backgrounds, beliefs, and traditions. As law enforcement leaders, it is crucial to recognize and embrace cultural differences, both within the agency and in the community, to build trust and ensure effective policing.

During my time as Chief of Police in both agencies, I learned that leading a diverse team requires cultural adaptability. It is not enough to have a strong command presence; you must also understand the people you are leading and the community you are serving. In both cities, my team and I implemented numerous community-oriented programs that took into account the specific needs and cultural backgrounds of the local population.

For example, in Simpsonville, we launched the *Neighborhood Traffic Calming Program*, which focused on neighborhoods where traffic issues disproportionately affected residents. Understanding the community's concerns and listening to feedback allowed us to tailor our approach to meet their needs. Similarly, the *Special Needs Assistance Program (SNAP)*, which I implemented in both Simpsonville and Laurens, was designed to assist families with special needs individuals. This program ensured that officers were educated on how to handle situations involving individuals with special needs in a respectful, compassionate, and effective manner. By knowing if a person had conditions such as dementia or autism, among other diagnoses, officers were able to respond with greater understanding and empathy, ensuring the best possible service to the community. Officers were informed of the individual's disability, where they lived, and any other relevant information the family wished to share, all of which helped ensure an appropriate response.

One of the most impactful initiatives was the *Cops Coaching Kids* program, which I introduced while serving as Chief of Police. The idea stemmed from recognizing the important role coaches have historically played in guiding and mentoring youth. We knew that many of the children we encountered in law enforcement came from single-parent households, lacking consistent male and/or female role models. Through this program, police officers volunteered their time to serve as coaches in local sports leagues, becoming mentors for at-risk youth. This program was incredibly successful in fostering positive relationships between law enforcement and the community. It allowed officers to build trust with young people in non-enforcement settings, showing them that police officers cared about their growth and well-being.

A striking example of the impact of this program occurred in Simpsonville, where I strongly believe it helped prevent a school shooting. Our School Resource Officers (SROs) not only coached sports like golf and basketball but were also actively involved in supporting local youth clubs. Their relationships with the kids were so strong that they were able to intervene in potentially deadly situations before they escalated. One morning, an SRO engaged in a routine conversation with a student who had recently been beaten up by a rival gang member. Unbeknownst to the officers, this student had brought a loaded gun to school that day, intending to carry out a mass shooting against his attackers.

The officers' genuine concern and rapport with the student had an unexpected and powerful impact. Later that day, the same student came into the SRO's office and handed over the loaded gun, admitting that he had planned to use it but couldn't go through with it because of the connection he felt with the officers. Their consistent engagement, through programs like *Cops Coaching Kids*, had built enough trust that the student felt he could turn to them instead of resorting to violence. This incident highlighted just how crucial these relationships can be in preventing tragedy.

Recognizing the rise of school shootings across the United States and understanding that bullying is a common denominator in many cases, we implemented an *Anti-Bullying Program*. This initiative aimed to address bullying, a significant factor in school shootings and childhood suicides, particularly within the LGBTQ+ community, where many recent shooters or suicide victims have identified. By intervening early and providing support to children who were being bullied, we hoped to reduce the likelihood of them turning to violence or self-harm as a response. The program started in elementary schools but also had components in middle and high schools, creating a continuum of support throughout all 12 years of education. Officers were trained to identify signs of bullying and provided with resources to work directly with schools, parents, and students. We knew that if we could prevent bullying, we might reduce the chances of future tragedies in our schools. The *Anti-Bullying Program* not only aimed to stop bullying but also sought to promote inclusion and respect among students, helping to create a safer and more supportive school environment for everyone.

Programs like these required an understanding of the unique cultural and social dynamics of the community. It wasn't about imposing a one-size-fits-all model but rather about adapting our methods to fit the needs of the people we served. In Laurens, for instance, we faced challenges tied to the city's racial history. By fostering open communication and trust with minority communities, we began addressing longstanding issues.

One example of this was our approach to *National Night Out (NNO)*. Before my arrival as Chief of Police, the community had not participated in NNO. Rather than making it solely about our department's relationship with the community, we transformed it into a county-wide event. We invited the Sheriff's Office, local police, state law enforcement agencies, EMS, the Fire Department, and other social services to participate. Our department spearheaded the planning and successfully secured over 35 vendors to provide free entertainment and giveaways. The event drew in thousands of citizens who were outwardly pleased to spend time with first responders in a fun, relaxed environment. This initiative not only created positive interactions between the public and law enforcement but also fostered greater unity across various community sectors, reinforcing our efforts to strengthen public safety through cooperation and mutual respect.

Adapting Leadership Style in Diverse Communities

It is not just in the community where cultural adaptability is important; within the department itself, cultural awareness plays a key role in leadership. The workforce in both Simpsonville and Laurens initially lacked diversity. We had to ensure that it consisted of officers with different racial, gender, and socioeconomic backgrounds to reflect the community they served. I worked to recruit a team that mirrored the diversity of the community.

For instance, while law enforcement has traditionally been male-dominated, I made it a point to increase the number of female and minority officers without lowering our hiring standards. By fostering an inclusive environment, we were able to attract candidates who might not otherwise have considered a career in law enforcement.

Once they are part of the team, it is essential to ensure that officers feel supported and valued. This is where programs like the *Employee Action Committee (EAC)* became invaluable. In both Simpsonville and Laurens, I met monthly with a representative from each shift and division to discuss any issues they were facing. These meetings opened up lines of communication and helped foster an open and inclusive environment. Officers knew they had a voice, and it strengthened morale when they saw that their input was valued. Additionally, we employed tools like anonymous employee surveys and a Chief's Suggestion Box, which further ensured open communication.

Cultural Adaptability in Crisis Situations

One of the most significant cultural challenges I faced in my career was during my time as the Senior Law Enforcement Advisor in Haiti, where I worked on rebuilding the Haitian National Police after the devastating earthquake. Haiti's cultural and political landscape was unlike anything I had encountered in the U.S., requiring me to adapt quickly. The people of Haiti had endured extreme poverty, political instability, corruption, and a lack of trust in law enforcement, which made policing incredibly complex. After my departure, the gangs in Haiti overtook the police force and assassinated the President, emphasizing the dire challenges the country faced.

While there, to gain the trust of the Haitian officers I was mentoring, I immersed myself in their culture and showed respect for their customs. This meant attending local events, learning some of the language, and understanding the historical context of their distrust in authority. By approaching leadership with cultural awareness, I was able to build stronger relationships and provide more effective guidance. This adaptability was critical to the success of the mission while I was there.

Back in the U.S., cultural sensitivity also came into play when leading my departments. For example, I had an officer on my staff from Palestine during the height of the Israel-Palestine conflict. This officer was very outspoken and vocal, as the situation directly affected her family members in the West Bank. I had to be sensitive to her feelings and her First Amendment right to free speech, while also ensuring I protected her and the department's reputation. It was essential that she avoided posting anything on social media that could be used against her or the department if she ever had to use force in the future, especially if the individual involved happened to be Jewish, pro-Israel, or held opposing views.

We met several times to discuss this, and she knew I genuinely cared about her and her family, which helped build trust. She took my advice to make her Facebook page private and to refrain from posting certain things that could create unnecessary complications down the line. This was a fine line I had to walk as a leader—to ensure I did not upset or insult her culture and beliefs, while also protecting her and the integrity of the department.

As part of the *Coffee with a Cop* program, I also made it a point to engage with members of the community in informal settings. These casual interactions helped break down barriers, especially in minority communities where trust in the police had been eroded over time. By simply listening and learning from the experiences of the community, we were able to improve relations and build a stronger bond between the police and the public.

The Importance of Recruiting a Diverse Workforce

Building a culturally diverse workforce that reflects the community is crucial in fostering public trust and improving law enforcement. In both Simpsonville and Laurens, I prioritized recruiting officers from various backgrounds. This wasn't about filling quotas; it was about creating a police force that could relate to and serve the community more effectively.

For example, we offered language incentive pay for officers who spoke more than one language. This allowed us to recruit multiple Spanish-speaking officers and others fluent in languages like Arabic and sign language. Having officers with these language skills enabled us to serve non-English-speaking residents more effectively and build stronger connections with different segments of the population.

Beyond recruitment, fostering an inclusive environment where officers feel supported and valued was essential. Through programs like the Police Explorer Program and the Reserve Officer Program, we attracted a wide range of candidates. We also created opportunities for mentorship to ensure new recruits had the guidance needed to thrive in their roles.

Valuing people is a fundamental aspect of leadership and recruitment. If you do not genuinely value people, you cannot add value to them. In every interaction, it's important to think about how you can add value to someone's day, whether it's through offering mentorship, encouragement, or providing opportunities for growth. This mindset fosters a culture of respect and support, which naturally attracts a diverse and talented team. When individuals feel valued, they are more likely to stay and invest in the organization, further strengthening its foundation.

Intentional and consistent effort played a key role in the success of these initiatives. Consistency compounds, meaning that the more regularly and deliberately you invest in building a diverse and inclusive workforce, the greater the long-term impact. This principle applies across all areas of leadership—whether in recruitment, team development, or cultural initiatives—because repeated, purposeful actions build momentum over time. The cumulative effect of being consistent is that it not only drives results but also strengthens the foundation of trust, inclusivity, and reliability within an organization.

In Laurens, we even expanded this approach to include local businesses through the *Law Enforcement and Business Coalition Against Nuisance*

Conduct. This program engaged local business owners and community leaders in addressing common problems in culturally sensitive ways. By collaborating with the business community, we developed solutions that enhanced crime prevention efforts and promoted a more inclusive approach to law enforcement.

By staying intentional and consistent in our efforts, and by valuing people, we created a culture that was not only diverse but sustainable, where trust, cooperation, and mutual respect continued to grow over time.

Adapting Leadership to Cultural Challenges in the Private Sector

The lessons I learned from adapting to cultural challenges in law enforcement also apply to leadership in the private sector. Whether you are leading a corporate team or a public organization, understanding the cultural dynamics of your workforce and customers is essential for success. A diverse team brings different perspectives, leading to innovative solutions and a more inclusive work environment.

In the private sector, cultural adaptability means recognizing the unique needs and expectations of your employees and customers. A company serving a global market must be sensitive to cultural differences in communication styles, work ethics, and customer service expectations. Just as I adapted my leadership style to fit the cultural context of the communities I served, corporate leaders must do the same to build trust and loyalty within their organizations.

For example, a corporate leader overseeing a multicultural team must be mindful of how different backgrounds influence work habits and communication. Some cultures may value collective decision-making, while others emphasize individual initiative. Understanding these nuances allows for a more cohesive and productive team environment.

Conclusion

Cultural adaptability is one of the most critical traits of an effective leader. Whether you are leading a police department, a corporate team, or an international organization, your ability to understand and navigate the cultural landscape around you will determine your success. In law enforcement, this means building trust with the community and creating an inclusive environment within the department. In the private sector, it means recognizing the diverse needs of your employees and customers and adjusting your leadership style to meet those needs.

By embracing cultural differences and adapting your leadership approach, you not only become a more effective leader but also build stronger, more cohesive teams that can work together to achieve common goals. In a world that is becoming increasingly interconnected, cultural adaptability is not just a skill—it is a necessity.

CHAPTER 12 : ADAPTING TO CULTURAL CHALLENGES

Reflect and Apply: Adapting to cultural differences is key to effective leadership in diverse environments. Reflect on how well you adapt your leadership style to different cultural contexts. Go to the **Appendix - Leadership Workbook and Action Plans** to document your strategies for leading diverse teams and building inclusive, culturally aware organizations.

CHAPTER 13:

LEADERSHIP AND TECHNOLOGY

Leadership today is not just about making decisions and managing people; it's about leveraging technology to enhance operations, improve efficiency, and stay ahead of evolving challenges. For law enforcement leaders, as well as executives in the private sector, understanding how to integrate technology effectively into daily operations is a crucial skill. The role of technology in leadership is to enhance, not replace, the human elements of empathy, judgment, and strategy that define great leaders.

Throughout my career over the last 26 years, I've witnessed the transformative power of technology in law enforcement, from data-driven policing to advanced investigative tools. But these lessons apply far beyond policing. The ability to harness technology is essential for any leader, whether in public service or in the private sector, and knowing how to implement it wisely is key to success.

Data-Driven Decision Making: Allocating Resources Effectively

One of the most powerful uses of technology in leadership is the ability to make data-driven decisions. In law enforcement, data analytics allows leaders to allocate resources where they are needed most, ensuring efficiency and improving public safety. During my time as Chief of Police, I saw firsthand how analyzing crime data helped us better understand crime patterns and predict future activity.

For example, when we implemented data-driven policing strategies in Simpsonville, we used crime data to identify hotspots where certain crimes were most likely to occur. This allowed us to strategically deploy officers to these areas, reducing response times and preventing incidents before they happened. Rather than responding reactively, we were able to take a proactive approach, which drastically reduced crime rates and optimized the use of our resources.

This same principle applies to the private sector. Business leaders can use data to identify market trends, predict customer behavior, and allocate resources to areas that will yield the most significant returns. For instance, companies can use data analytics to track sales performance, measure customer engagement, and identify areas of improvement. Just as law enforcement leaders must rely on data to make informed decisions, corporate leaders must harness data to gain insights that lead to smarter, more efficient operations.

AI: The Present and Future of Leadership

Advancements in Artificial Intelligence (AI) have revolutionized decision-making processes in ways we could not have imagined even a decade ago. AI technology allows data to be processed and analyzed in a fraction of the time it once took, enabling leaders to make more informed decisions with unprecedented speed and accuracy. What used to require weeks of analysis can now be done in seconds with AI-powered tools. In law enforcement, AI can identify patterns in criminal activity that humans might miss, helping to allocate resources even more precisely and preventing crime before it happens.

For modern leaders, embracing AI is not optional—it is imperative. Those who fail to integrate AI into their leadership strategy risk being left behind. AI is the key to staying competitive, efficient, and adaptable in a rapidly changing world. In government, AI is already being used for predictive policing, emergency response planning, and resource allocation. Beyond law enforcement, AI is improving decision-making across sectors, from healthcare, where it helps with diagnostics and patient care, to city planning, where it optimizes traffic flow and energy consumption.

In the corporate world, AI is essential for leaders who want to remain ahead of the curve. Companies that utilize AI to forecast market trends, optimize supply chains, and provide real-time insights into business performance have a distinct advantage over those that rely solely on human analysis. AI can improve customer service through chatbots, automate routine tasks, and help companies understand customer preferences in ways that were previously impossible. Leaders who adopt AI can drive innovation, reduce inefficiencies, and make smarter decisions faster than ever before.

AI is the now and the future of leadership. Whether in government or the private sector, leaders must understand that AI is not just a tool—it is a fundamental shift in how decisions are made and how organizations operate. Those who embrace AI and integrate it into their leadership approach will be better equipped to meet the challenges of tomorrow. Those who don't will quickly find themselves outpaced by competitors or unable to meet the increasing demands of their constituents.

In both the public and private sectors, the most successful leaders of tomorrow will be those who can blend human judgment with AI's analytical power, using technology to complement intuition and experience. AI allows leaders to focus on strategic decisions, while the technology handles the heavy lifting of data processing and forecasting.

Embracing AI not only enhances efficiency but also frees leaders to focus on innovation, creativity, and the human side of leadership—traits that will remain irreplaceable even in an AI-driven world.

License Plate Readers: A Force Multiplier for Law Enforcement

One of the most impactful pieces of technology we implemented while serving as Chief of Police was the use of License Plate Readers (LPRs). These systems scan and capture the license plates of passing vehicles, comparing them against databases of stolen cars, wanted persons, and other flagged alerts. LPRs work around the clock, providing law enforcement with real-time data and alerts even when officers aren't physically present in an area.

LPRs were a force multiplier for our department, allowing us to monitor high-traffic areas without needing an officer on site at all times. This technology played a critical role in reducing crime rates and solving a variety of cases, including locating missing persons such as Alzheimer's patients who had wandered away from home and gotten lost. In Laurens, LPRs helped us recover stolen vehicles and identify suspects involved in serious crimes, making the community safer and freeing up officers for other pressing tasks.

In business, similar technologies like automated systems and machine learning algorithms can operate continuously to optimize processes and workflows, multiplying the effectiveness of a small team. Just as LPRs allowed us to cover more ground without increasing manpower, automation in business can reduce labor costs, improve accuracy, and increase output—all without sacrificing quality.

Office of Investigative Technology: Leveraging Digital Evidence

Technology has fundamentally changed the way we investigate crimes, especially with the integration of digital tools. As Chief of Police, I launched the Office of Investigative Technology, a specialized unit designed to handle complex technological aspects of investigations. One of the most significant breakthroughs came with the ability to extract data from cell phones and electronic devices. This data often provided critical insights into a suspect's mindset and actions, leading to quicker case resolutions.

Cell phones, in particular, became treasure troves of evidence. Suspects might delete messages, clear their browsing history, or try to hide incriminating information, but our digital forensic tools could recover these details. The evidence we extracted often proved so damning that it led to plea deals, preventing long, drawn-out court battles. In turn, this helped relieve the burden on the judicial system, ensuring that cases moved swiftly through the courts.

Current technologies, such as facial recognition and the ability to match images across social media platforms, have become indispensable in identifying unknown suspects. We can now use technology to monitor a person's body language or facial expressions during interviews or interrogations to assess the probability of deception. While this type of technology is not yet admissible in court, it can be a powerful investigative tool to confront a suspect and further a criminal investigation.

As technology evolves, law enforcement must continuously adapt and utilize it to the best of our abilities. Leaders in law enforcement, as well as the private sector, need to stay ahead of these advancements, using them ethically and strategically to make informed decisions.

In the private sector, business leaders can apply this lesson by leveraging technology to gain insights into customer behavior, competitor strategies, or operational inefficiencies. Just as digital evidence reveals hidden truths in law enforcement, data analysis in business can uncover patterns and opportunities that aren't immediately apparent. The ability to use technology to gather and interpret valuable data is a key leadership skill, whether you're managing a police department or a corporation.

Integrating Technology into Daily Operations

The success of any technological initiative depends on how well it is integrated into daily operations. As Chief of Police, I oversaw the upgrade of in-car computer systems, ensuring that officers had access to critical information while on patrol. This improved response times and enhanced officer safety by providing them with up-to-date crime reports, maps, and suspect information.

In the business world, leaders face similar challenges when integrating new technologies into their organizations. Whether it's upgrading software systems, implementing cloud-based solutions, or adopting new communication tools, leaders must ensure that technology enhances daily operations without overwhelming the workforce. Effective integration requires training, support, and a clear vision of how the technology will improve the organization's overall performance.

For example, when we updated all the patrol cars with new computers, it wasn't just about purchasing new hardware. We had to train officers on how to use the systems effectively, troubleshoot issues, and ensure that the new technology fit seamlessly into their workflow. Similarly, in the private sector, introducing new technology requires thoughtful planning and leadership to ensure employees embrace it and use it to its full potential.

The Ethical Use of Technology

While technology offers significant advantages, its use comes with ethical responsibilities. In law enforcement, this is especially true when it comes to surveillance, data collection, and privacy concerns. For example, body-worn cameras have become essential tools for accountability and transparency, but they also raise questions about privacy, data storage, and the potential for misuse.

As a leader, it's crucial to strike a balance between leveraging technology for public safety and respecting individual rights. The same is true in the business world, where companies collect vast amounts of personal data from customers and employees. Leaders must establish clear ethical guidelines for how this data is used, ensuring that technology enhances operations without compromising trust or violating privacy laws.

Ethical leadership in technology involves not only setting policies but also fostering a culture of transparency and accountability. In law enforcement, we established strict protocols for how and when body cameras were used, ensuring that officers understood the importance of respecting the privacy of the public while maintaining the integrity of our operations. Similarly, in business, leaders must be proactive in establishing data protection policies and ensuring compliance with regulations.

The Human Element: Technology and Empathy

As powerful as technology is, it can never replace the human element of leadership. Empathy, judgment, and personal connection remain at the heart of effective leadership. Technology can assist in making data-driven decisions, improving efficiency, and enhancing operations, but it's the human interactions that truly define leadership.

Every person and situation is unique, and no machine can replicate the empathy required to understand and address the needs of individuals. In law enforcement, this is especially true in the way officers interact with the public. No amount of data or technology can replace the trust and relationships built between officers and the communities they serve. The same holds true in the business world, where customers, employees, and stakeholders want to feel valued and heard, not simply managed by algorithms and systems. While AI and automation can streamline processes, leaders must remember that human connection is irreplaceable. Whether managing a police department or running a corporation, technology is a tool, but empathy, integrity, and genuine human engagement remain the foundations of great leadership.

Conclusion: Balancing Technology with Human Leadership

Technology is an essential tool for modern leaders, whether in law enforcement or the private sector. It offers unprecedented opportunities to improve efficiency, conduct strategic planning, make data-driven decisions, and solve complex problems. However, successful leaders know that technology alone is not enough. It must be balanced with the human elements of leadership—empathy, judgment, and ethical decision-making.

In both public service and business, leaders who can effectively integrate technology into their operations while maintaining a strong human connection will be best positioned to succeed. As technology continues to evolve, leaders must remain adaptable, thoughtful, and, above all, grounded in the values that define great leadership. While the tools of the future may change, the core principles of leadership will remain constant: integrity, empathy, and a commitment to serving others.

CHAPTER 13 : LEADERSHIP AND TECHNOLOGY

Reflect and Apply: Technology is transforming leadership. Reflect on how you can better leverage technology while maintaining the human element in your leadership. Use the **Appendix - Leadership Workbook and Action Plans** to document ways to incorporate technology in decision-making, communication, and organizational efficiency while staying grounded in empathy.

CHAPTER 14:

ETHICS AND LEADERSHIP

In leadership, ethics is not just a set of guidelines—it is the foundation upon which all decisions and actions are based. Throughout my career in law enforcement, I have been confronted with situations that tested my moral compass and required me to make difficult choices. These experiences have reinforced my belief that ethical leadership is paramount, particularly in roles that hold significant power and influence over others. When you're at the top, every decision you make is scrutinized, and maintaining unwavering ethical standards is crucial for the success and integrity of the organization you lead.

Ethical Challenges Faced During My Time as Chief of Police

Serving as a two-time Chief of Police provided some of the greatest ethical tests of my career. These moments required difficult decisions, often in the face of political and personal pressure, and highlighted the difference between being a leader who merely speaks about integrity and one who acts on it, regardless of the consequences.

In Simpsonville, one of the most defining moments came when I was asked by the mayor to overlook violations of the law and unethical behavior by high-ranking police officers and other city officials. I was faced with a choice: turn a blind eye or pursue the truth, no matter the personal cost. Choosing the latter was not easy; it meant risking my career by going against powerful individuals who held influence over the city. However, I knew that compromising my ethics would betray the very principles I had committed to upholding and were ingrained in me from my upbringing.

The decision to pursue the truth initially cost me my job. I was terminated for blowing the whistle on corruption, and the weight of that decision hung over me for the next 14 months. Yet, in the end, justice prevailed. For over a year, a group of citizens protested this injustice. Eventually, a newly elected majority on the city council reviewed my termination, determined it to be unlawful, and reinstated me as Chief of Police with full backpay. This led to indictments and convictions for public corruption involving the mayor and other high-ranking officials. It was a victory for ethics, but it also placed a mark on my career that I have had to explain at every subsequent opportunity. Even though my actions were ultimately vindicated, having a termination on your record remains a challenge. However, I've learned that those who disqualify me for doing the right thing are not the kind of people I would want to work for or with in the first place.

In Laurens, I faced another ethical dilemma when multiple officers came forward about misconduct by a member of my leadership team. The allegations included off-duty criminal behavior and a culture of unethical practices perpetuated by this individual dating back years prior to my time as Chief of Police. Again, I conducted a thorough investigation, which led to the uncovering of even more violations. Despite receiving advice from city officials to terminate the individuals involved, political intervention ultimately led to me no longer being Chief of Police. Once again, doing the right thing came at the cost of my position. But I sleep peacefully knowing that I upheld the integrity of the role, even when those around me were determined to preserve corruption and cover up what was going on.

One recurring theme I have encountered throughout my career is the pressure that comes from those in power to avoid confrontation or unpleasant truths. Being a Chief of Police is not for someone looking to coast through their career, preserving their position by doing little to upset the status quo. It requires bold action, moral courage, and the willingness to bring old, festering issues to the surface—even at the risk of losing your job. Unfortunately, many leaders choose not to rock the boat, content to leave things as they are. This is why you see some Chiefs of Police remain in their positions for decades without creating any lasting change.

Just because a Chief of Police has held a position for a long time does not automatically mean they are a great leader. Longevity in leadership can sometimes indicate a reluctance to confront challenges or make difficult decisions. Some leaders may prioritize job security over what is right, avoiding systemic problems within their departments in order to maintain favor with those in power. Their legacy may fade with their retirement, as they are remembered for playing it safe rather than taking meaningful stands.

On the other hand, there are many chiefs who serve long tenures with unwavering integrity, never compromising their values or ethics. These leaders manage to avoid the pitfalls of political pressure while still fostering positive change and maintaining high ethical standards. It's important to acknowledge that while their paths may have been different, they earned their longevity through principled leadership.

However, it is highly unlikely that many of them encountered the same crossroads I have, where politicians implied or directly asked that they overlook unethical or illegal behavior in exchange for job security. When you face these kinds of situations, you learn quickly that doing the right thing comes at a cost. The difference is that some leaders choose the easy route to keep their positions, while others take the harder path, knowing that true leadership is measured by standing up for what is right, even if it means risking everything, not by how long you hold a position.

Keen Sense of Justice in Leadership

A keen sense of justice is something that cannot be taught—it is often ingrained in the DNA of a true leader from a young age. This internal compass, guiding an individual to stand up for others and for what is right, starts early and continues throughout life. As children, we find ourselves standing up to bullies, protecting those less fortunate, and defending others when no one else will. This innate drive for fairness and justice shapes our character and determines the type of leaders we will become.

For me, this sense of justice was evident from an early age. Growing up, I found myself getting into a lot of fights—not because I enjoyed fighting, but because I was always standing up for someone or something I believed in. I couldn't just turn the other cheek when I saw others being mistreated. There was a righteousness in my approach, and I never fought for the sake of it. I was defending what was fair, just, and right. As I grew older, this never wavered. People who knew me as a child and those who know me as an adult often say I haven't changed—I've always been driven by a need to stand up for others. In many ways, I was predestined to become a police officer, a role that perfectly aligned with my lifelong commitment to fighting for the rights of others.

This sense of justice isn't only about fighting or defending people—it's about knowing when to act and when to exercise restraint. As a leader, you must have the wisdom to determine when to utilize this ingrained sense of fairness and justice in decision-making. A balanced approach, where fairness, justice, and self-control converge, is critical for building an organization that thrives on respect and trust. It's not enough to simply know what is right—you have to act on it while maintaining control of your temper, desires, and emotions.

Throughout my career, self-control has been as important as my sense of justice. Being a leader doesn't just mean standing up for what's right—it means doing so with integrity, without letting emotions drive your decisions. Maintaining control over your temper, your desires, and even your appetite for success is key to effective leadership. This self-discipline keeps you grounded and ensures that your actions align with the ethical values you promote.

As a child, my sense of justice was raw and unfiltered, often expressed through physical actions. However, as I matured, I came to understand that true leadership demands more than righteous anger—it requires a thoughtful, measured approach to making decisions that are both fair and just. The ability to maintain self-control while passionately defending what is right is what distinguishes great leaders. It's a delicate balance, but one that is crucial for fostering a strong, ethical organization. These skills are developed by practicing integrity in private, which will later serve you in public. In other words, it's about your character—doing what is right whether others are watching or you are alone.

This deep-seated sense of justice—coupled with self-control and ethical decision-making—has defined my leadership journey. It has guided me through difficult times, allowing me to stand firm in my convictions, even when the cost was high. Leaders with this innate sense of fairness are those who build trust, foster loyalty, and create lasting legacies. The foundation of any great leader lies in their ability to do what is right, at the right time, with the right balance of justice and restraint.

Ethics Extend Beyond Being Chief of Police

These ethical challenges are not confined to being a Chief of Police. I have seen many ethical dilemmas in my roles abroad and as a special agent or investigator. Throughout these experiences, I always chose to do what was right, and in those roles, my actions were praised. For example, the fact that I took a stand against corruption in Simpsonville—leading to convictions of both politicians and police officers—helped me land top leadership roles in three different countries.

Working abroad in Haiti, Liberia, and Afghanistan, ethics were a focal point of my mission, and the commitment to integrity was often praised at the international level. I appreciated how, in those contexts, standing up for what was right was met with respect and rewarded with further opportunities. Yet, it is ironic that in my domestic leadership roles as Chief of Police, taking the same ethical stance hindered my career growth. It often feels as though the very integrity that earned me international acclaim became a liability in local law enforcement, perhaps because police chiefs are appointed by elected officials—some of whom do not always have the public's best interests at heart.

Despite these challenges, my belief in ethical leadership has remained unwavering. I know that I cannot control everything or everyone, but I take comfort in the fact that I have always done the right thing. If the corrupt individuals I encountered during my time as Chief of Police are never held accountable here on earth, I am confident they will face judgment before God. As it says in the Bible, "Vengeance is mine; I will repay, says the Lord" (Romans 12:19). I know that these individuals will one day have to answer for their actions, and that gives me peace.

Personal Ethics and Professional Integrity

Ethics in leadership are not confined to professional responsibilities. In my time as Chief of Police, I adhered to the belief that personal integrity directly influences professional conduct. I had a motto: if you cheat on your spouse, the person you swore an oath to under God, you are likely to do bad things at work as well. Whether it's backdating a report, falsifying documents, or covering up a crime, a lack of personal ethics often leads to professional misconduct. This standard was made clear within my departments, and it became a cornerstone of the ethical culture we built.

Leaders who lack personal integrity—those who cheat, lie, or deceive in their personal lives—are more likely to act unethically in their professional roles. When a supervisor or higher-up tells you they don't care what people do off duty, you know you're dealing with someone who lacks the moral compass necessary for ethical leadership. These individuals are likely to look the other way or cover up misconduct when it suits their interests, and that's where a clash with a Chief of Police who values ethics inevitably arises. In a world that seems to be eroding in terms of values and ethics, standing firm in your beliefs, even when it costs you, is a hallmark of true leadership.

Conclusion: Ethical Leadership as a Legacy

As you continue on your leadership journey, remember that ethics is the cornerstone of true leadership. It is not just about avoiding wrongdoing but about standing for what is right, even when it's unpopular or inconvenient. Your actions as a leader set the tone for your entire organization, and the legacy you leave behind will be defined by how you lead.

While taking a stand may cost you in the short term, it is the only path to building a lasting legacy of integrity. Ethical leadership is not for the faint of heart, but it is the only way to ensure that your leadership leaves an enduring impact. Lead with ethics at the forefront, and you'll not only build a stronger, more resilient organization but inspire others to follow in your footsteps.

CHAPTER 14 : ETHICS AND LEADERSHIP

Reflect and Apply: Ethical leadership defines your legacy. As you complete this chapter, reflect on the ethical challenges you've faced and how you've responded to them. Head to the **Appendix - Leadership Workbook and Action Plans** to document your ethical principles, assess recent decisions, and plan for how you'll continue to lead with integrity.

CHAPTER 15:

NAVIGATING ORGANIZATIONAL POLITICS

As a leader, particularly in public service roles like that of a Chief of Police, navigating organizational politics is a critical skill that can significantly impact your success and effectiveness. It's essential to manage these dynamics without compromising your integrity, staying focused on your primary responsibility: serving the people, regardless of their political affiliations.

Appearing Neutral and Serving Everyone

Throughout my tenure as Chief of Police, I made it a point to remain politically neutral and focus solely on serving the entire community. My role as Chief was not to align with any political party but to ensure public safety for everyone. Law enforcement is not about politics; it's about addressing the needs of the community. Whether the issue was a call for help or a community initiative, I always handled it without allowing any political considerations to influence my judgment.

This neutrality allowed me to gain the respect of most politicians, as they understood that I was there to do my job with integrity and fairness. However, I did clash with a few who attempted to pull me into unethical situations or asked me to compromise my values for political reasons. In those cases, my refusal to align with political influences became a shield against potential misconduct, and those who were unethical quickly learned that I was not someone who could be swayed by backroom deals or underhanded tactics. Unfortunately, by not siding with corrupt politicians, it sometimes appeared as though I was politically aligned with those who were ethical and opposed corrupt individuals. As a result, despite my best efforts to remain neutral, it often seemed that I had inadvertently taken a political side by default.

Another one of the critical lessons I learned, especially during my early years as Chief of Police, is how your public and personal life can be intertwined in the eyes of the community. In my first role as Chief of Police, it was during a highly contested time in law enforcement, compounded by the intensity of a presidential election. Like many, I believed that what I posted on my personal Facebook page, separate from my role, wouldn't impact my position. However, I quickly learned that it doesn't matter if it's on a personal page—everything you post can be used against you.

People who disagree with you, particularly those who may not favor law enforcement, will seize any opportunity to weaponize your words against you. A single political post or personal opinion, no matter how unrelated to your professional duties, can be taken out of context and used to discredit your integrity or the neutrality you work hard to maintain as a leader. In my case, the fallout from a few personal posts was enough to teach me how crucial it is to maintain a clear separation between personal views and public service.

Based on this experience, I always advise fellow leaders to clean up their social media presence. Keep your personal profiles private, limited to a small circle of close friends or family. Even with those settings, I recommend avoiding political posts or anything controversial. I understand it can be challenging, especially in a world where everyone has an opinion and a platform to share it, but the risks far outweigh any potential reward. As a leader in law enforcement or the private sector, your reputation is one of your greatest assets, and protecting it means avoiding unnecessary controversies that can arise from social media.

In law enforcement, when someone dials 911, we don't ask for their political affiliations before we act. We risk our lives for the safety of strangers without any consideration of their background, beliefs, or affiliations. It's crucial that your social media presence reflects the same neutrality. Giving anyone ammunition to question your impartiality can lead to public doubt. Even if the reality of your actions and intentions is different, a past post or comment can be twisted to make it seem like you're biased or acting out of personal agenda.

Another key point to remember is that trying to defend yourself or explain away a misunderstood post often leads to losing the battle in the public eye. Once the damage is done, trying to clarify your position through social media or in public forums usually only exacerbates the situation. A simple misunderstanding can turn into a larger issue that detracts from your role as a leader. In today's connected world, it's vital to be cautious with every message you put out there, whether it's a social media post, email, or public statement.

Neutrality in Leadership

This principle of neutrality is not confined to law enforcement; it's essential in the private sector as well. Whether you're running a police department or a corporation, serving all stakeholders equally is a critical aspect of leadership. Leaders in the private sector can learn from this example by focusing on the mission of their organization and remaining committed to fairness, even when faced with political or financial pressures that might tempt them to deviate from their values.

Ultimately, whether you are navigating public service or the corporate world, maintaining neutrality and avoiding political entanglements helps build trust. Your community, employees, and stakeholders need to believe that you are there to serve everyone equally, without bias. By avoiding political discourse and maintaining a neutral, fair, and balanced approach, you create an environment where your leadership can thrive, free from unnecessary controversies.

Knowing the Hills You're Willing to Die On

One of the most important lessons I've learned as a leader is knowing the "hills" worth standing firm on, even at great personal risk. Integrity is non-negotiable. Twice in my career as Chief of Police, I stood my ground against political pressure to overlook bad acts committed by police officers, knowing that doing so could cost me my job. But these were moments that defined my leadership and set the tone for the ethical standard I expected from my officers and from myself.

Standing up for what's right—whether it's in law enforcement, politics, or business—requires courage. Leaders must know in advance where they draw the line, and they must be prepared to face the consequences of those decisions. Compromising your core values for the sake of keeping a position is not leadership; it's self-preservation. I've always believed that the right fight, no matter how difficult, is worth it if it protects the integrity of the organization and its mission.

In both the public and private sectors, these "hills" will look different. In business, it could be refusing to engage in unethical marketing practices, while in law enforcement, it could be standing against corruption. Whatever the challenge, knowing your non-negotiables allows you to lead with clarity and conviction.

Balancing Political Needs with Integrity

One of the realities of leadership, especially in public roles, is that you can't completely avoid political considerations. In law enforcement, rebranding initiatives or partnerships with community leaders often involved collaboration with politicians. While some compromises are inevitable, the challenge lies in drawing the line between harmless political concessions and those that compromise your integrity.

During my time as Chief, I made small concessions where they didn't harm the department's integrity—things like collaborating on community events or taking input from elected officials on non-critical matters. However, on significant ethical issues, I remained firm. Striking this balance is critical in leadership. Even in the private sector, there will be moments where business leaders must engage with political stakeholders or board members with differing views. The key is to maintain integrity without alienating key partners.

Transparency: A Double-Edged Sword

Transparency is often touted as an essential leadership trait, but it can be a double-edged sword, particularly in law enforcement and public service. Throughout my tenure as Chief of Police, I prided myself on being open about the realities of law enforcement, whether it involved efforts to crack down on drug traffickers, pedophiles, or violent offenders. This transparency built trust with the community but sometimes clashed with the interests of local politicians. They preferred to project an image of a serene, crime-free town to attract residents and businesses- a mindset I refer to as the "Andy Griffith Show" or the "Mayberry" approach. While appealing, we all know this is not a realistic portrayal of the challenges we face in today's world.

One of the most important lessons I learned was to be wary of politicians who publicly advocate for transparency but privately express discomfort when information conflicts with their preferred narrative. In both positions as Chief of Police, I encountered elected officials who outwardly supported transparency but, behind closed doors, questioned my decision to release certain details. Their concerns weren't based on public safety or departmental integrity but rather on how the information might impact the city's image or economic interests. One mayor, in particular, instructed me—and had the city administrator tell me—to "use my time more wisely" than by arresting pedophiles who didn't live in our city but came here to prey on our youth. The reality was that they disliked the proactive police work because it brought attention to pedophile arrests within our community. Instead of recognizing that our department was actively protecting children by conducting undercover operations to catch predators targeting our youth, they focused solely on how this could negatively affect the city's reputation.

While we could have compromised by doing fewer press releases, they instead told me to stop making these types of arrests altogether. I felt that this approach put our children at even greater risk than they already faced from the predators lurking on social media.

During my time as Chief of Police in Laurens, I took great pride in being more transparent than my predecessors. We used social media as a powerful tool for community engagement, increasing our Facebook followers by over 400%. By the time I left, we had more followers than the total number of citizens in the city. This growth was significant because it demonstrated the community's trust in us and their desire to stay informed. We shared both the good and the bad, offering a real-time look into the proactive police work we were doing through stings, arrests, and community outreach.

However, after I left, the new administration adopted a much more guarded approach, only sharing positive community stories and the occasional crime update in reaction to major incidents. The growth on social media stopped completely, and transparency diminished, which I later found out was a direct order from the mayor to the next chief. This shift concerned me deeply, especially when I learned of five drive-by shootings in the area and a kidnapping with an active manhunt that were never publicized or communicated to the community. I discovered these incidents when assisting agencies posted about their involvement in the manhunt, and police officers who responded to the scenes directly informed me about the shootings. Failing to alert the public not only keeps them in the dark but also limits their ability to assist in investigations or take necessary precautions. Real-time sharing of information is crucial for public safety, as it enables citizens to work alongside law enforcement in locating suspects and staying vigilant. As public servants, we have an obligation to inform the taxpayers—the people we serve—about the realities of crime in their community. If we don't, how can we justify requests for more funding or special equipment in future budgets?

Failing to maintain transparency as a Chief of Police means you have compromised your ethics and the citizens' right to know about crime in their community, all in an effort to keep your position. In the law enforcement world, we call this type of Chief a "yes man," someone who simply follows orders without standing up for what is right. These individuals have zero respect among their peers. People may listen to them out of fear of punishment, but not because they respect them as true leaders.

What's even more troubling is how many people are deceived by this type of Chief—especially the citizens, who may perceive them as a nice, approachable person without realizing the cowardice behind their actions. The community often fails to see that, by refusing to stand up for transparency and failing to warn the public about potential dangers, this type of Chief has compromised their safety. Their fear of upsetting political figures or damaging their own career leads them to withhold critical information, which ultimately puts the community at risk. When a leader prioritizes self-preservation over the safety of the people they are sworn to protect, the whole community suffers the consequences.

The same lesson applies in the private sector. Transparency can build strong relationships with stakeholders, but there's always a tension between being open and protecting the organization's image. Too much transparency can sometimes expose vulnerabilities that can be exploited or misinterpreted, while too little can breed suspicion and damage trust. As a leader, striking the right balance is critical, and it often comes down to being honest about the risks and challenges without unnecessarily harming the organization's reputation.

Ultimately, transparency in leadership is about building trust and maintaining integrity. It's not about creating a perfect image; it's about being real with the people you serve and lead. In my experience, when you're open about the challenges you face—whether it's a spike in crime or a tough business decision—it gives you the credibility to ask for support, whether that's from your community, your board of directors, or your employees. When transparency is handled ethically, it becomes one of the most powerful tools a leader has to inspire trust and foster cooperation.

Fairness and Perception

Fairness goes beyond simply treating people equally; it's also about managing how others perceive that fairness. During my time as Chief, it was critical to treat my officers and the community with respect and fairness, ensuring everyone felt valued. However, people's perception of your fairness is just as important as the reality. They need to believe that you're willing to go the extra mile for them, even if you cannot always meet their demands. In public leadership, this perception of fairness builds trust, credibility, and loyalty.

In the private sector, managing perception is equally crucial. Employees, customers, and partners all need to feel that they are being treated fairly and that you are working in their best interests. Effective leaders know how to communicate in ways that reinforce this perception, fostering a sense of mutual respect and trust.

Navigating the Political Landscape

Successfully navigating organizational politics involves building strategic relationships and understanding the power dynamics at play. This doesn't mean playing political games but rather knowing when to stand firm and when to compromise. One of the challenges I faced early in my career as a Chief of Police was handling unethical politicians who tried to pull me into compromising situations. In these moments, I took a very rigid, hard-line approach, which, while rooted in my strong sense of ethics, might have been handled with more finesse.

As a brand-new chief, I was deeply committed to upholding the law and maintaining my integrity. So, when I was first asked to overlook criminal and ethical violations by some of the city's political figures, my immediate response was an absolute, unwavering "no." I took this stance because I was shocked by the request and felt cornered. Having spent six years in undercover narcotics, where temptations and ethical dilemmas were constant, I prided myself on never being swayed. But my rigid response in this situation may have been more driven by emotion and the feeling of being set up than by a strategic approach to resolving the issue.

Looking back, I realize that a more measured response could have helped me navigate the situation without drawing a hard line in the sand so quickly. While I never regretted taking a stand for what was right, I learned that how you take that stand is just as important as the stance itself. In my eagerness to defend my ethics, I might have alienated potential allies or closed off channels for discussion that could have led to a more effective solution.

Instead of immediately lashing back with an uncompromising refusal, I now believe that I could have handled the situation differently by shielding my initial emotions. Taking a softer approach doesn't mean compromising your values; it means creating space for dialogue, buying time to assess the situation fully, and working behind the scenes to address the problem. Had I shielded my emotions and quietly reported the issue to a federal agency like the FBI or a state law enforcement division, I might have been able to protect my integrity without creating such immediate conflict.

It's critical for leaders to strike a balance between standing up for what's right and maintaining relationships. A rigid response, while well-intentioned, can sometimes shut down avenues for resolution and escalate conflicts. In retrospect, I see that a softer, more strategic approach would have allowed me to continue fighting the same battles but perhaps with fewer personal repercussions.

This lesson isn't exclusive to law enforcement. In the private sector, leaders often face situations where they must protect their integrity while navigating a politically charged environment. Knowing when to take a firm stand and when to apply a more diplomatic touch is key to long-term success. You can still hold your values without alienating others or burning bridges prematurely. In fact, flexibility and emotional intelligence are essential in preserving those relationships that might help you bring about the change you're fighting for in the long run.

In both public and private sectors, leaders face complex political landscapes. Knowing when to engage, when to withdraw, and how to align your goals with the interests of various stakeholders can make or break your success. At times, it's not enough just to be right—you have to be strategic in how you approach ethical dilemmas. Being rigid can backfire, while navigating politics with a sense of flexibility allows you to maintain your integrity while working toward lasting solutions.

The Importance of Strategic Communication

Effective communication is one of the most powerful tools a leader possesses. Throughout my career, I've learned that strategic communication is about more than just delivering information—it's about crafting messages that align with your values, resonate with your audience, and are conveyed in a way that maintains the integrity of your organization. Whether addressing the public, interacting with politicians, or communicating with your own team, your messaging must be clear, consistent, and intentional to foster trust and credibility.

One critical aspect of strategic communication is understanding that how you say something can be just as important as what you say. The tone, medium, and timing of your message can drastically affect how it's received. This is especially true in sensitive situations where miscommunication can lead to misunderstandings or escalate conflicts. In the business world, just as in law enforcement, leaders must communicate with a variety of stakeholders, including employees, customers, and shareholders, in a way that inspires action and builds confidence in the organization's direction. The goal is not only to inform but to create a sense of alignment between the leader's vision and the audience's needs.

Beware of Misunderstandings in Digital Communication

One of the lessons I've learned in leadership is the importance of being mindful of the tone in written communication, particularly in press releases, emails, and text messages. In the fast-paced world of law enforcement, or in any business, it's tempting to keep messages short and to the point. However, concise or blunt communication, while efficient, can sometimes be misinterpreted as curt, angry, or dismissive. When a message lacks context or warmth, it leaves room for people to read between the lines—often incorrectly.

I've personally fallen victim to my bluntness being misunderstood. My goal was often to provide clarity and efficiency, but the unintended consequence was that my tone came across as harsh or impatient. For example, I once sent a short response to an email where I was trying to confirm details quickly, but my brevity led others to believe I was upset, which wasn't the case at all. It's a delicate balance: while it's important to be clear and direct, taking a moment to include a brief sentence to soften your tone can go a long way in preventing miscommunication.

In press releases, for instance, every word matters. The public often reads between the lines, and a poorly crafted statement can spark unintended controversy. This is why it's essential to have multiple eyes review all public-facing communications before they go out. Ideally, someone trained in public relations or media should assess these messages to ensure that they're accurate, clear, and reflect the values and image you want to project. Having a trusted public information officer, or someone skilled in communications, review your press releases can save you from potential misunderstandings that might arise from unclear or hastily written statements.

Context Matters in Strategic Communication

In leadership, context is critical to strategic communication. Understanding your audience allows you to tailor your message to fit their expectations and the situation. For example, when addressing your team, you might want to be more detailed and transparent than when speaking to the public, who may not need the same level of specificity. Politicians, on the other hand, often require diplomatic phrasing that addresses their concerns while aligning with your own goals.

Equally important is mastering the details in leadership. Much like an intricate machine, every part of an organization must function cohesively, and a leader must ensure that all components are working effectively. This requires not only a deep understanding of the big picture but also a mastery of the finer details that keep the system running smoothly. A strong leader ensures that backup systems are in place so that if something goes wrong, the entire operation doesn't come to a halt. This level of detail-oriented leadership prevents small issues from escalating into major problems and keeps the organization agile and resilient.

Mastery of details extends to communication itself. The medium of communication plays a significant role in ensuring that your message is not only understood but also conveyed in the right tone. Text messages and emails are useful for quick updates or logistical matters but are rarely appropriate for delivering sensitive or complex messages. These forms of communication lack tone and nuance, which can lead to misinterpretation. Whenever possible, delivering important or sensitive messages face-to-face or through a phone call ensures that you can manage tone and gauge reactions in real time. This allows for immediate clarification if something is misunderstood, helping to prevent escalation.

Leadership demands not only a strategic vision but also an attention to the smaller components that ensure that vision is executed effectively. When leaders focus on the details and ensure that all parts are working as they should, they build an organization that can withstand challenges and maintain momentum toward its goals.

Strategic Communication in Crisis Situations

In times of crisis, strategic communication becomes even more essential. How you communicate during a crisis can shape the public's perception of your leadership and the organization. Leaders must be transparent but also calm and composed. This can be a challenging balance, as it requires you to provide enough information to keep people informed while not causing unnecessary panic.

In my time as Chief of Police, we faced several critical incidents that required a steady hand in communicating with the public. Whether it was a crime wave, a major arrest, or a significant event in the community, we had to ensure that our messaging was not only transparent but also reassuring. People look to leaders for stability, especially in uncertain times. A poorly crafted message can undermine confidence, while a well-thought-out response can strengthen trust and build unity.

This principle applies equally in business. During challenging times, such as a financial downturn, product recall, or negative press, how a leader communicates can either exacerbate the situation or help mitigate the damage. Clear, honest, and measured communication reassures stakeholders that the organization is taking the appropriate steps to address the issue, which can preserve—and even strengthen—your reputation in the long run.

Mastering the Art of Communication

Mastering the art of strategic communication means continually refining your ability to convey the right message to the right audience, at the right time, and through the right medium. Whether in the public or private sector, successful leaders must be able to engage effectively with their teams, stakeholders, and the wider community. This means being thoughtful, not only about the information you are sharing but also about how it is delivered.

Clear, consistent, and intentional communication builds trust and maintains credibility—key factors in navigating organizational politics and leading effectively. For those aiming to polish their leadership skills, understanding how to manage the nuances of communication can make a world of difference. From choosing your words carefully to being mindful of your tone, every aspect of communication plays a role in defining your leadership style and your ability to inspire those around you.

Conclusion: Leadership Beyond Politics

Leadership, at its core, transcends the realm of politics. While navigating organizational politics is a critical skill, true leadership is about maintaining integrity, fostering trust, and guiding people through challenges. The ability to stay grounded in your principles while strategically engaging with stakeholders is what sets effective leaders apart. Whether in public service or the private sector, the same fundamentals apply—remain steadfast in your commitment to fairness, transparency, and ethical communication.

In my career as Chief of Police, I learned that although political influences will always be present, they must never define your leadership. The real test of leadership comes when you are forced to choose between political expediency and doing what is right. How you handle those moments will determine the long-term impact of your leadership.

In both public service and the business world, the most successful leaders are those who stay true to their values, no matter the pressure. This doesn't mean being inflexible or unwilling to compromise when appropriate—it means knowing the boundaries of what you are willing to compromise and ensuring that those boundaries are grounded in integrity.

Moreover, leaders who rise above politics by consistently prioritizing the well-being of their team, their community, and their organization will leave behind legacies that go far beyond their tenure. As you continue on your leadership journey, remember that success is not just about navigating the power dynamics around you but about ensuring that your actions are always in service of the greater good.

True leadership is measured not by how well you play political games but by how effectively you steer your organization with integrity, empathy, and a commitment to lasting positive change. The lessons learned in managing organizational politics, whether in law enforcement or the corporate world, are universal. Ultimately, the most powerful form of leadership is one that rises above the fray, remains committed to ethical principles, and inspires others to do the same.

CHAPTER 15 : NAVIGATING ORGANIZATIONAL POLITICS

Reflect and Apply: Navigating politics while maintaining integrity is a key leadership skill. Reflect on how you handle organizational politics and ensure your actions align with your values. Go to the **Appendix - Leadership Workbook and Action Plans** to document strategies for balancing political dynamics with ethical leadership.

CHAPTER 16:

ENCOURAGING POSITIVE CULTURE THROUGH CELEBRATING SUCCESSES

Creating a positive organizational culture is one of the most impactful things a leader can do. A culture that recognizes and celebrates success not only boosts morale but also fosters loyalty, motivation, and a sense of belonging among team members. Throughout my career, I've seen firsthand how a simple acknowledgment of hard work can transform an individual's attitude and inspire an entire team to strive for excellence.

The Power of Recognition

While many claim they don't work for accolades, the reality is that recognition matters. Being appreciated for our contributions fulfills a fundamental human need. When leaders take the time to acknowledge the efforts of their team members, it reinforces a culture of appreciation and respect. Recognition should be genuine and meaningful. If done right, it strengthens bonds between leadership and the workforce, boosting motivation and reinforcing positive behavior.

In my leadership roles, I have made it a point to prioritize recognition. My strategy has always been to "flood" personnel files with commendations rather than criticism. This approach not only uplifts morale but also provides balance when constructive feedback or discipline is necessary. An employee with numerous commendations in their file will not feel discouraged by a single write-up, knowing that their overall contributions are highly valued.

Celebrating Successes Without Overdoing It

While it's essential to celebrate successes, it's equally important not to dilute the value of recognition by overdoing it. If every minor achievement is met with lavish praise, recognition risks becoming meaningless. Leaders must find a balance between acknowledging great work and ensuring that recognition remains meaningful.

Tailor your recognition to match the significance of the accomplishment. A major achievement may warrant public recognition in a meeting, while a smaller contribution might be best acknowledged with a simple "thank you" or a personal note. This ensures that employees feel their contributions are valued appropriately without creating an atmosphere of complacency.

Transforming the Personnel File

In many organizations, personnel files are often viewed as a place to document negative incidents—warnings, write-ups, and disciplinary actions. However, I believe that personnel files should tell a more complete story, showcasing an employee's positive contributions alongside any areas for growth. Filling these files with commendations and praise helps to build a more balanced picture of performance, offering a powerful tool during evaluations or promotions.

This approach not only serves as a testament to an employee's dedication but also fosters a culture of encouragement. When employees see their hard work documented and valued, they feel more connected to the organization. This kind of recognition builds loyalty, showing that the organization invests in its people beyond disciplinary measures.

Building Loyalty Through Caring Leadership

Recognition is an important part of leadership, but genuine care for your team is what truly builds loyalty. When employees feel that their leaders care about them not only as workers but as individuals, they are more likely to give their best effort. Caring leadership is about more than just praising good work; it's about listening to concerns, offering support in times of need, and helping individuals grow both personally and professionally. Taking the time to understand the challenges your team members face and providing resources for their development shows that you are invested in their success. This trust is the foundation of a healthy organizational culture. Leaders who demonstrate this type of care often find that their team members will go above and beyond, not out of obligation but out of genuine loyalty.

One of the greatest gifts a leader can give is the gift of attention. By giving someone your full attention, you show that you genuinely care about them and their concerns. In the end, people won't necessarily remember what you said during a conversation, but they will remember how you made them feel. This applies not only to your team members within an organization but also to your customers in any business setting. Attention is powerful—it signals respect and value.

As Chief of Police, this approach was particularly effective when citizens came to file a complaint about an officer. Often, people come in frustrated or upset, and simply sitting down, listening to them, and giving them your undivided attention can be enough to remedy the situation. In many cases, the complaint itself wasn't as important as the individual feeling heard and understood. Just by giving them time and attention, I could de-escalate emotions and show that their concerns mattered to me personally. This same principle applies in any business. Whether you're leading a team or dealing with customers, the way you make people feel by giving them attention builds trust and loyalty. When people know they are being heard, they are more likely to engage positively and contribute to the success of the organization. It's not just about resolving complaints or problems; it's about creating a lasting connection that demonstrates you care beyond the transaction.

In the end, the loyalty and trust that come from genuinely caring about others, paying attention, and building strong relationships are what truly drive long-term success in any organization.

Fostering a Culture of Excellence

Creating a positive culture through recognition is about more than just celebrating wins—it's about fostering a culture of excellence. This culture is built by setting clear expectations, providing the support needed to achieve them, and recognizing the hard work that goes into meeting those expectations. But to be effective, recognition must be consistent, fair, and based on merit.

A culture of excellence thrives on continuous improvement. Leaders must encourage ongoing development, offer opportunities for learning, and set the example by continuously striving to improve their own leadership skills. When everyone in the organization is encouraged to be their best, a positive culture of high performance naturally follows.

The Power of Pushing Beyond Comfort Zones

In the pursuit of excellence, there are moments when leaders must push their teams to perform at maximum capacity, often taking them beyond their comfort zones. This can be a challenging experience for both the leader and the team, as it often involves embracing change, confronting fears, and stepping into unknown territory. However, those who trust the leadership and follow the direction will often impress not only their superiors but themselves. Pushing people outside of their comfort zones is a powerful way to identify future leaders. In my experience, those who rise to the occasion and tackle difficult tasks with enthusiasm and determination are the ones who have the potential to take on greater leadership roles in the future. These individuals often show qualities of resilience, adaptability, and innovation, which are essential for effective leadership.

However, not everyone is willing to push through the discomfort required for growth. Some may become disgruntled, resist change, or even speak negatively about leadership when they are confronted with challenges that force them to evolve. It's important to recognize that not everyone has what it takes to achieve greatness, and many are simply unwilling to get uncomfortable to grow. For those individuals, change can be frightening, and their resistance to stepping outside their comfort zone often prevents them from reaching their full potential.

On the other hand, those who accept the challenge of growth and thrive in high-performance environments are the ones worth investing in. These individuals show themselves as the future leaders of the organization, and it's a joy to watch them rise to the top. They demonstrate a willingness to embrace the hard work and dedication it takes to achieve success, and as a leader, it's incredibly rewarding to spend extra time mentoring and guiding them toward their goals.

Creating a Lasting Impact

Leadership isn't just about achieving results—it's about building a legacy. When leaders focus on celebrating successes, recognizing contributions, and fostering a caring culture, they create an environment where individuals are motivated to achieve more. This not only improves performance in the short term but also builds a sense of belonging and commitment that extends beyond any single project or task. In the public and private sectors alike, leaders who celebrate successes foster environments that retain talent and maintain high levels of engagement. In the business world, this can lead to increased productivity, innovation, and customer satisfaction. In law enforcement or public service, it means stronger community relations, improved morale, and greater success in meeting organizational goals.

Encouraging Growth While Maintaining Balance

While pushing your team to excel is critical, it is equally important to maintain balance. Growth is uncomfortable, but it must be managed thoughtfully. A leader must recognize when to push and when to pull back. Those that are growing require encouragement, guidance, and recognition to keep striving. Creating an environment where discomfort leads to growth, and success is celebrated, fosters both personal and organizational development.

In conclusion, building a positive culture through recognition and celebration isn't just a feel-good strategy; it's a powerful leadership tool. When done correctly, it inspires loyalty, encourages growth, and leads to the long-term success of both individuals and organizations. As a leader, your responsibility is to recognize the effort and dedication of your team, fostering a culture that celebrates success, embraces growth, and encourages continuous improvement.

CHAPTER 16 : ENCOURAGING POSITIVE CULTURE THROUGH CELEBRATING SUCCESSES

Reflect and Apply: Recognizing and celebrating success fosters a positive culture. Reflect on how you can better celebrate your team's successes without overdoing it. Head to the **Appendix - Leadership Workbook and Action Plans** to outline strategies for fostering a culture of recognition, motivation, and growth within your organization.

CHAPTER 17:

FACING ADVERSITY IN LEADERSHIP

Introduction: Resilience and Growth Through Adversity

Adversity is an inevitable part of leadership, and how we respond to challenges defines our effectiveness. Throughout my career, I've faced numerous obstacles—both expected and unforeseen—that tested my resolve, creativity, and resilience. Overcoming adversity is not just about surviving difficult situations but about learning from them and emerging stronger on the other side. Leaders in any field must confront adversity head-on, adapt, and grow through the process.

Standing on Integrity: Ethical Leadership in the Face of Challenges

One of the most significant challenges I faced was during my time as Chief of Police in Simpsonville. I was wrongfully terminated after refusing to compromise on ethical standards. My commitment to holding officers accountable and standing against corruption led to my termination, despite being rooted in integrity. I fought a 14-month legal battle to regain my position, eventually winning reinstatement. The experience reinforced the importance of standing firm on ethical principles, even when it results in personal or professional adversity.

During this period, I had to deal with political pressure and public backlash, but I never wavered from my commitment to doing the right thing. The lesson here is universal: integrity in leadership can be a double-edged sword. Standing on ethical grounds can result in conflicts with stakeholders, but in the long run, it is the bedrock of sustainable leadership. This applies across industries—whether you're leading a corporate team or a government agency, integrity fosters trust, stability, and long-term respect.

Resilience in the Face of Challenges: The Role of Support Systems and Personal Strength

During my legal battle, my support system was crucial. Family, friends, and colleagues helped me stay grounded and strong through the challenges. Their unwavering belief in my character gave me the strength to keep going, even when doubt crept in.

Resilience doesn't just stem from personal strength, though—it often depends on those around you. The sacrifices my family made during this time were significant, reminding me that leadership adversity affects everyone in your circle. When you take a stand, it's your family and support system that endures the strain alongside you.

In law enforcement, corporate America, or any leadership role, resilience is vital. It's what allows leaders to confront adversity, adapt to challenges, and maintain focus on their mission despite difficulties. Leadership is not about avoiding adversity, but about confronting it head-on and refusing to let it define you.

Navigating Public Criticism with Resilience and Integrity: Leadership Under Public Scrutiny

Leadership often brings with it a level of visibility and, inevitably, public criticism. During my time as Chief of Police, I faced intense public scrutiny. A newspaper even compared me to a mob boss, portraying me as a problem rather than someone trying to fix a corrupt system. My personal and professional reputation came under heavy fire as critics sought to discredit me.

At first, I fought back, trying to prove my critics wrong. But over time, I realized the importance of focusing on the bigger picture—my actions, leadership, and commitment to service—rather than getting entangled in the noise. A wise friend advised me that "no press is bad press in the long run," and I shifted my energy from defending myself to taking positive actions that spoke for themselves.

This lesson is applicable across sectors. Whether you're leading a company or a police department, how you respond to public criticism defines you as a leader. Focusing on your mission and letting your positive impact be your response is a lesson in resilience that applies to all leaders.

In corporate America, CEOs are often at the mercy of public opinion, media scrutiny, and shareholder pressure. The key is not to get entangled in short-term battles but to stay focused on the bigger picture. Staying calm, composed, and empathetic, even when facing criticism, sets a strong example for your team and helps maintain stability.

Operation Good Time: Leadership in the Face of Political Pressure

One of the most defining moments of my career came during Operation Good Time, a human trafficking and prostitution sting that gained national attention. This operation was unique in that we leveraged social media to work undercover and identify individuals involved in prostitution and human trafficking. Over the course of 12 hours, we arrested 54 individuals, including key figures involved in trafficking rings. The mission wasn't just about making arrests—it was about rescuing victims from dangerous and exploitative situations.

Despite the operation's success, the political fallout was severe. Just days after the sting, I was forced to choose between resigning or facing termination. Certain politicians felt that I had made the town look like it had a human trafficking problem, and they wanted me out. Their priority wasn't addressing the real issue at hand but protecting the town's image, as though ignoring the problem would make it disappear. It's a sad reflection of the world we live in, but this is the reality and the consequence of electing people who do not truly represent the will of the community they are supposed to serve.

Knowing the risk to my career, I still moved forward with the operation because it was the right thing to do. Rescuing human trafficking victims was not something I could ignore or delay for the sake of job security. It would have been easier to do nothing, to slide under the radar, and preserve my position for the long term, but I'm not that type of leader. I don't procrastinate or shy away from tough decisions when people are being victimized. This was a hill I was willing to die on.

True leadership is about doing what's right, even when the personal cost is high. If you are the kind of leader who looks the other way when faced with difficult choices, you need to take a hard look in the mirror. If you're not willing to act when action is required, especially when lives are at stake, then you are either incompetent or in the wrong position. Leadership is about stepping up when it matters most, not retreating into self-preservation.

Even though I was being forced to resign, my priority was to honor my officers for their bravery and dedication during Operation Good Time. In my final hour before resigning, instead of seeking pity or badmouthing what was being done to me, I scrambled to complete my last act as Chief: hand-delivering letters of commendation to those involved in the operation. I made sure these letters were permanently placed in their personnel files to send a clear message—what they did with this operation was commendable and deserved formal recognition. This experience solidified my belief that true leadership isn't about protecting your position—it's about standing by your people and doing what is right, no matter the consequences. Ethics and integrity should never be second-guessed in leadership. If you are driven by fear or the desire to keep your job at all costs, you have already failed as a leader.

CHAPTER 17 : FACING ADVERSITY IN LEADERSHIP

Reflect and Apply: Adversity shapes great leaders. Reflect on the challenges you've faced in your leadership journey and consider how you responded to them. Did you stand on your principles, even when it was difficult? How did your support system and resilience play a role in overcoming adversity? Think about ways to continue developing resilience and ethical leadership as you navigate future challenges. To deepen your reflection, use the **Appendix – Leadership Workbook and Action Plans** to document key lessons learned from past adversities and create strategies for handling future obstacles with a mindset of growth and integrity.

CHAPTER 18:

THRIVING THROUGH ADVERSITY

Dynamic Leadership and Political Realities: Adapting Leadership in an Unstable Environment

As a dynamic change-agent leader, I often found myself at odds with political realities. Leaders like myself, who push for significant reforms and hold high standards, face resistance in environments resistant to change. In Simpsonville, I worked under four different mayors and 12 separate council members over four years, creating a highly unstable environment.

In corporate settings, dynamic leaders face similar challenges when driving progress in organizations that are resistant to change. Balancing the pace of change with political and organizational realities requires adaptability and strategic leadership. Learning to slow down and navigate political waters is essential to achieving long-term success while maintaining a bold vision for progress.

Navigating Leadership and Relationships: Trust and Loyalty in Leadership

Leadership attracts people—some with genuine intentions and others with self-serving motives. I learned this the hard way when I helped a long-time friend get elected as sheriff, only for him to distance himself once in office. His isolation from those who provided honest feedback, combined with unethical decisions, eventually led to his arrest and conviction on public corruption charges.

This experience taught me the importance of surrounding yourself with people who genuinely have your best interests at heart. Leaders in any field must be cautious about who they trust. True loyalty is rooted in integrity, and allowing the wrong people into your inner circle can destroy not only your career but also your integrity.

The Challenge of Scrutiny and Shortened Tenures: Adapting to Modern Leadership Realities

In today's environment, the tenure of Chiefs of Police has significantly decreased, largely due to increased scrutiny and public accountability. Similar trends are seen in corporate America, where CEOs face shortened tenures due to media pressure, public opinion, and shareholder expectations.

Leaders in both law enforcement and corporate settings must adapt to this reality, understanding that scrutiny is part of the job. While this can be daunting, focusing on ethical decision-making and transparency helps leaders weather the storm. Those who thrive understand that their tenure is not defined by its length, but by the impact they make during their time in leadership.

Learning from Setbacks: Turning Adversity into Leadership Growth

Every setback I encountered throughout my career was an opportunity for growth. During my legal battle, I used the time to reflect on my leadership, refine my skills, and stay engaged with the law enforcement community. When I was reinstated, it wasn't just a personal victory—it was a win for the principles I stood for.

Leaders in all industries should embrace setbacks as part of the leadership journey. Adversity provides the opportunity to reassess, grow, and emerge stronger. It's not the setback itself that defines leadership—it's how you respond to it. Remaining adaptable and resilient, even in the face of failure or rejection, is key to overcoming obstacles and continuing to move forward.

Maintaining a Positive Outlook

Another key aspect of overcoming adversity is maintaining a positive outlook, even when things seem bleak. During my time in international law enforcement roles, I encountered incredibly difficult situations, such as dealing with the aftermath of natural disasters in Haiti and navigating post-conflict environments in Liberia. In these moments, it was easy to become overwhelmed by the enormity of the challenges. However, I learned that focusing on what could be done—no matter how small—was crucial for moving forward. By setting achievable goals and celebrating small victories, I maintained momentum and inspired my team to keep pushing forward.

In any leadership position, focusing on small, achievable goals during challenging times is vital. Whether in law enforcement, corporate leadership, or any other field, celebrating incremental progress helps build morale and keeps teams moving toward the larger mission.

Turning Setbacks into Opportunities

Leadership is not defined by ease but by how we respond to adversity. In my leadership journey, I've learned that every setback is an opportunity to grow, to sharpen my skills, and to become a more effective leader. The challenges I've faced have only strengthened my resolve, and I've come to understand that true leadership is about embracing these challenges, standing firm on your values, and refusing to be defined by adversity.

As you encounter adversity in your leadership journey, remember that these challenges are not roadblocks—they are stepping stones to becoming a stronger, more effective leader. Embrace the lessons that adversity offers, lean on your support network, and never lose sight of your core values. In doing so, you will not only overcome the challenges before you but also inspire others to do the same.

Conclusion: Lessons on Resilience from Adversity

Adversity is not a roadblock—it's a stepping stone to becoming a more effective leader. The challenges I've faced have only strengthened my resolve, and true leadership is about standing firm on your values and embracing those challenges. Whether you're leading a law enforcement agency, a corporation, or a non-profit, the lessons of resilience, integrity, and adaptability are universal. Stay focused on your mission, and let adversity fuel your growth as a leader.

CHAPTER 18 : THRIVING THROUGH ADVERSITY

Reflect and Apply: Thriving through adversity requires resilience, adaptability, and a commitment to your core values. Reflect on how you've handled setbacks and public scrutiny in your leadership role. How have these experiences shaped your leadership style, and what lessons can you take forward? Consider the importance of surrounding yourself with the right people and maintaining a positive outlook, even in the face of challenges. Use the **Appendix – Leadership Workbook and Action Plans** to document your key takeaways from navigating adversity and outline how you can turn future setbacks into opportunities for leadership growth and success.

CHAPTER 19:

TRANSITIONING LEADERSHIP ACROSS INDUSTRIES

Leadership principles transcend industries. Whether you're transitioning from law enforcement to corporate America, moving from the private sector into public service, or seeking to adapt your leadership skills across different roles, the core competencies that define effective leadership remain the same. My transition from law enforcement, where I spent 26 years, including roles as Chief of Police and contractor for the U.S. Department of State, to corporate leadership opened my eyes to the universality of these skills. Though the environments differ, the ability to lead with integrity, manage crises, and build effective teams is essential across any field.

This chapter explores how transferable leadership skills apply across different industries, including law enforcement and the private sector. Whether you're looking to adapt your leadership style in a new role or build your capacity to lead diverse teams, these lessons provide insight into navigating leadership transitions.

Understanding the Parallels Between Law Enforcement and Corporate Leadership

At first glance, law enforcement and corporate leadership may seem worlds apart, but there are significant parallels. In both fields, leaders must manage teams, oversee budgets, ensure compliance, and maintain public or stakeholder relations. The skills honed in one environment often translate seamlessly to another.

For example, as Chief of Police, managing risk and maintaining organizational structure were part of my daily routine. Ensuring that proper protocols were followed in high-stakes situations parallels corporate leadership, where risk management is crucial for business success. This skill applies to leaders overseeing operations, legal compliance, or safety measures in any corporate role.

Corporate leaders are often tasked with ensuring compliance, mitigating risks, and developing strategic plans that keep the organization on track. Whether you're managing a team in healthcare, finance, technology, or logistics, the ability to assess risks and put safeguards in place is invaluable. In business, just like in policing, small missteps in protocol or oversight can have wide-reaching consequences.

By drawing on your leadership experience in managing complex, high-pressure situations- whether in law enforcement, corporate security, or crisis management- you're equipped to navigate the demands of any industry.

Transferable Leadership Skills: From Law Enforcement to Corporate America (and Beyond)

Crisis Management: Staying Calm Under Pressure

One of the most important leadership skills that transcends industries is crisis management. In law enforcement, crises often demand split-second decisions in life-or-death situations. Similarly, in corporate America, leaders are regularly tasked with managing high-stakes issues such as product recalls, market downturns, or reputational crises.

In both settings, the leader's response to a crisis sets the tone for the entire team. While crises in corporate settings may not always involve immediate physical danger, the stakes—such as financial stability, company reputation, or employee safety—can be just as high. Remaining calm under pressure is a skill that every leader needs, regardless of the environment.

Imagine you're leading a team in a healthcare company, and a product fails quality standards. The public's trust in your brand is at risk, and the business could face regulatory penalties. The way you handle this situation will impact both your internal team and external stakeholders. Leaders who can stay composed, assess the situation, communicate effectively, and provide clear direction will gain the trust of both their team and the market. This parallels how police officers must remain calm during an emergency, ensuring that order is maintained even in chaotic circumstances.

In any industry, the ability to stay calm under pressure not only guides your team but also reassures clients, customers, and other stakeholders that you are in control of the situation.

Decision-Making and Accountability: Leading With Integrity

In law enforcement, leaders make critical decisions that impact public safety, and they must be prepared to stand by those decisions. Accountability is fundamental to building trust in both law enforcement and corporate leadership. Leaders who own their decisions and take responsibility for their outcomes foster trust within their teams and with the people they serve.

This same principle applies in the private sector. Leaders must make tough calls, often with incomplete information, and accept responsibility for the outcomes, whether they lead to success or require adjustment. Making ethical decisions and standing by them builds a culture of integrity that strengthens the entire organization.

In a corporate environment, decision-making is key to achieving goals and driving the organization forward. Whether you're an executive leading a product development team, a manager overseeing financial decisions, or a department head responsible for hiring, you must make decisions with confidence and be accountable for their results. Leaders in retail, manufacturing, tech, and even nonprofits benefit from clear, decisive action paired with transparency.

Taking responsibility for both successes and setbacks is essential in leadership. Whether you're managing a law enforcement team or a corporate project, owning the outcome fosters respect and accountability at every level.

Building and Leading Effective Teams in High-Stress Environments

In both law enforcement and corporate leadership, the ability to build and lead effective teams is a critical component of success. In law enforcement, leaders must give orders that are followed immediately. In the corporate world, leadership often requires a more collaborative approach, fostering innovation and encouraging input from across the team.

However, at the heart of both styles is the same goal: motivating people to work toward a shared objective. Strong leaders in any sector understand the importance of building trust, empowering their teams, and fostering a culture of respect and collaboration.

Whether you're managing a tech startup, overseeing operations in a hospital, or leading a team in a large corporation, you need to know how to bring people together, guide them toward common goals, and get the best performance out of each individual. This involves not only setting clear expectations but also creating an environment where team members feel valued and supported.

Leading in the corporate world, just like in law enforcement, means understanding that your success depends on your team's success. Leaders must establish strong communication, provide consistent feedback, and foster a sense of ownership and accountability within their teams.

Integrity and a Clear Background as Cornerstones of Leadership

Integrity is universally valued in leadership. In law enforcement, integrity is paramount, as officers are entrusted with upholding the law and public safety. Similarly, in the corporate world, leaders must demonstrate ethical decision-making and transparency, whether dealing with financials, compliance, or team management.

Maintaining a strong sense of integrity, combined with holding others accountable, is essential for building a culture of trust in any organization. Leaders who demonstrate fairness and uphold ethical standards will inspire confidence, both within their teams and across their industries.

In any industry—whether finance, tech, healthcare, or manufacturing—integrity is a cornerstone of leadership. Ethical business practices, transparency in decision-making, and fairness in holding employees accountable are critical components of building a sustainable organization. For instance, a leader in finance must ensure compliance with regulations, avoid conflicts of interest, and prioritize the trust of clients and investors. Just like in law enforcement, integrity in corporate settings earns long-term loyalty and trust, which ultimately drives success.

Whether you're leading a large corporation or a small business, the foundation of your leadership is built on integrity.

Outlets Outside of Work: Maintaining Work-Life Balance

One of the most valuable lessons I learned in transitioning to corporate leadership was the importance of having outlets outside of work. Law enforcement can often be all-consuming, especially in leadership positions like Chief of Police. Similarly, corporate executives often face high-pressure environments that require round-the-clock dedication. Without personal interests, hobbies, and family time, burnout becomes a real possibility.

Whether you're an entrepreneur, a corporate leader, or in law enforcement, finding balance is critical to maintaining long-term effectiveness. For example, many successful leaders in business, like those in tech or finance, take up hobbies such as fitness, writing, or family activities to maintain mental clarity. This balance helps leaders recharge, gain perspective, and bring their best selves to work every day.

It's essential to cultivate interests outside of your professional identity to prevent burnout and maintain a healthy work-life balance. Just as physical fitness, family time, and hobbies helped me navigate transitions in my career, these activities can be key to your success in any leadership role.

Compensation and Work-Life Balance: Understanding the Trade-Offs

While corporate roles tend to offer higher salaries than many public service jobs, such as law enforcement, the benefits must be weighed against other factors like work-life balance and job satisfaction. In corporate America, while the pay is often higher, it may come with volatility and uncertainty, as layoffs and economic downturns can impact job security.

Leaders in the private sector, from retail and healthcare to finance and manufacturing, must consider how compensation aligns with personal fulfillment and work-life balance. High salaries can be attractive, but leaders should also evaluate the stability, personal fulfillment, and long-term growth potential of a role. The balance between professional success and personal well-being is crucial for long-term satisfaction and productivity.

Understanding the trade-offs between compensation, work-life balance, and job stability is essential in making informed career decisions, whether in the public or private sector.

Corporate to Command Staff: Reverse Transitions and Cross-Industry Leadership

While much of this chapter has focused on transitioning from law enforcement to corporate America, the reverse transition is equally valuable. Corporate professionals bring important skills such as strategic planning, financial management, and stakeholder engagement to public service roles, including command staff positions in law enforcement or government agencies.

For example, corporate leaders often have deep experience in budgeting, long-term planning, and managing relationships with key stakeholders. These skills are just as valuable in law enforcement, where police chiefs and command staff must ensure that resources are allocated efficiently and that the department's objectives align with community needs.

Corporate professionals transitioning into leadership roles in public service can leverage their strategic thinking, financial management, and stakeholder engagement skills to enhance the efficiency and effectiveness of public agencies. Whether entering law enforcement or another government agency, the leadership skills developed in the private sector are highly transferable to the public domain.

Conclusion: Leadership Adaptability Across Different Environments

Leadership transcends specific industries, whether law enforcement, corporate America, or any other field. The key skills of integrity, decision-making, crisis management, and team-building are universally applicable across all leadership roles. Transitioning between industries offers the opportunity to adapt and apply these core principles in new ways, creating well-rounded, effective leaders.

For any leader—whether you're moving from corporate to public service, law enforcement to business, or managing teams across various sectors—the ability to adapt your leadership style to new challenges is what sets you apart. Stay grounded in your core values of integrity, accountability, and service, and you will succeed in any environment.

CHAPTER 19 : TRANSITIONING LEADERSHIP ACROSS INDUSTRIES

Reflect and Apply: Leadership skills are universally transferable across industries. Reflect on the key leadership traits discussed in this chapter, such as crisis management, decision-making, and team-building, and consider how they apply to both your current role and potential future roles in other sectors. Turn to the **Appendix - Leadership Workbook and Action Plans** to document how you can leverage your existing leadership skills for cross-industry success, identify areas for further development, and create a strategic plan for adapting your leadership style to new environments.

CONCLUSION:
THE LEGACY OF LEADERSHIP

Leadership is not a title or position—it is a lifelong journey of growth, learning, and service. As we've explored in this book, the true measure of a leader is found in the principles they uphold, the challenges they overcome, and the impact they leave on the people and communities they serve.

Throughout my career in law enforcement, whether on the streets of the U.S. as a police officer or working undercover as a Special Agent with the U.S. Drug Enforcement Administration, to navigating the challenging environments of Afghanistan, Haiti, and Liberia, I have learned that leadership is about more than just making decisions or giving orders. It is about leading with integrity, navigating crises with calm and clarity, building strong and effective teams, demonstrating consistency, and always putting the needs of the community at the forefront. It is about understanding and respecting the diverse cultures and perspectives that make up our world, and it is about staying resilient in the face of adversity.

But perhaps most importantly, leadership is about legacy. The decisions we make, the values we uphold, and the way we treat others—all of these contribute to the legacy we leave behind. My hope is that the lessons and experiences shared in this book will inspire you to lead with purpose, compassion, and unwavering ethical standards.

As you move forward in your leadership journey, remember that every challenge is an opportunity to grow, every setback is a chance to demonstrate resilience, and every decision is a reflection of your values. Lead with integrity, serve with humility, and strive to make a positive difference in the lives of those you lead.

In the end, the legacy you build as a leader is not just about the accomplishments you achieve, but about the lasting impact you have on the people and communities you serve. It is my sincere hope that you will take the lessons from this book and use them to build a legacy of leadership that you—and those who follow you—can be proud of.

Thank you for embarking on this journey with me, and I wish you all the best as you continue to lead with purpose and passion. If you read and apply any of the skills from this book to advance your career, please share your experience by writing an Amazon review. We hope that by sharing your stories, others can learn even more. Everyone has something to teach, and you never know how your experiences may resonate and help others unless you put them out there for the world to read.

Conclusion: The Legacy of Leadership

Reflect and Apply: Leadership is about the legacy you leave behind. Reflect on the lasting impact you want to make through your leadership. Use the **Appendix - Leadership Workbook and Action Plans** to outline the steps you'll take to build a legacy defined by ethical, compassionate, and purposeful leadership.

BONUS SECTION: PERFECTING THE INTERVIEW TO LAND THE POSITION YOU DESIRE

Securing a leadership position—whether in law enforcement or the private sector—often hinges on how well you perform in the interview. Your resume may open the door, but it's the interview that solidifies your spot as the best candidate. Excelling in an interview means balancing confidence with humility, presenting yourself professionally, and demonstrating how your experience adds value to the organization. Whether you're applying for a Chief of Police role or a senior position in the corporate world, your ability to provide specific examples of your leadership experiences is key to setting yourself apart.

This section offers insight for both law enforcement and corporate candidates, providing examples relevant to both areas.

1. Confidence vs. Arrogance

Confidence is crucial in any interview, but it's important to distinguish between confidence and arrogance. Confidence means you believe in your abilities, can articulate your qualifications clearly, and are prepared to discuss your experiences openly. Arrogance, however, can come off as dismissive or self-important. Striking the right balance ensures that the interview panel sees you as capable and open to collaboration.

In law enforcement, confidence means clearly demonstrating your ability to make tough decisions under pressure, such as in crisis management or high-stakes operations. For example, when interviewing for a Chief of Police position, I often talk about my experience leading an undercover investigation that resulted in dismantling a human trafficking ring connected to a major drug cartel. However, I always emphasize the role of teamwork and collaboration, making sure to credit the success to the broader team effort.

In the private sector, leaders must similarly project confidence, but with a focus on results-oriented achievements such as driving business growth, increasing efficiency, or innovating new solutions. A senior executive might share how they led their team through a successful product launch or a merger, but balance that with recognizing the contributions of their colleagues. Confidence, combined with humility, shows that you are both results-driven and a team player.

2. Turning Negatives into Positives

Every leader faces challenges, but how you frame these experiences can make all the difference in an interview. Rather than avoiding difficult situations, see them as opportunities to showcase your resilience, problem-solving abilities, and capacity for growth.

In law enforcement, challenges may include public criticism or handling sensitive situations. For example, during an interview, I often address a time when I faced public scrutiny as Chief of Police. I reframed the situation by discussing how it strengthened my crisis management skills and improved community relations through transparency and open dialogue.

In the corporate world, leaders frequently encounter difficult market conditions, budget constraints, or internal conflicts. For instance, a business leader might explain how they guided a company through a major financial downturn by implementing cost-saving measures and increasing efficiency, ultimately positioning the organization for long-term success. Whether in law enforcement or business, the ability to take responsibility for past challenges and demonstrate how you've grown from them is a hallmark of strong leadership.

3. Dressing the Part

Your appearance plays a significant role in creating a strong first impression. Dressing appropriately for the position you're applying for is essential, whether it's a formal suit in law enforcement or more business-casual attire in corporate settings. Understanding the company or department's culture will help you gauge the right look.

In my own experience, applying for a Chief of Police position taught me how even small details in appearance can influence perceptions. For corporate interviews, the same principle applies. A well-tailored suit for an executive-level position—often referred to as a "C-suite role" (which includes CEO, CFO, or other high-ranking executives)- signals professionalism and readiness for leadership. Alternatively, a more relaxed, yet polished, look may be appropriate in industries that prioritize creativity and innovation.

The key is to align your appearance with the organization's expectations, ensuring you look the part and are perceived as someone who can step into a leadership role seamlessly.

4. Greeting the Panel

First impressions are crucial, and greeting the interview panel with warmth, professionalism, and confidence sets the tone for the rest of the interview. In law enforcement, a firm handshake, direct eye contact, and addressing each panel member by name help establish rapport, signaling that you are approachable and serious about the role.

For a corporate leadership interview, your goal is the same—build rapport by acknowledging the panel, engaging them with direct but friendly eye contact, and demonstrating confidence without being overbearing. Making the interview feel more conversational rather than stiff and overly formal can put everyone at ease and help the panel see you as someone they could easily work with.

5. Asking Insightful Questions

Asking thoughtful questions during the interview is essential to demonstrating your interest in the organization. In law enforcement, you might ask, "What challenges is the department currently facing, and how do you see this role contributing to solutions?" This shows that you're already thinking strategically about how you can help improve the department.

In the private sector, asking questions about the company's growth strategy, market challenges, or how success in the role is measured positions you as someone who is not only interested in the role but also thinking long-term. For instance, asking, "What are the key performance indicators for success in this role?" or "How does this company approach innovation in a rapidly changing industry?" shows you're forward-thinking and eager to make a meaningful impact.

6. Be Well-Groomed

In both law enforcement and corporate interviews, personal grooming is critical. A polished appearance—whether it's clean-shaven or a well-maintained beard, trimmed hair, or appropriately styled attire—reflects your professionalism and attention to detail. In one of my own experiences, my appearance in an interview was commented on negatively, even though I thought I looked well-groomed. I learned the importance of adapting to what the interviewers expect and aligning my appearance accordingly.

For corporate roles, grooming matters just as much. If you look well-presented and organized, it reassures interviewers that you take pride in your professional image and will represent the company well.

7. Research and Preparation

Research is fundamental to preparing for any leadership interview. In law enforcement, you need to understand the department's crime rates, current challenges, and recent initiatives. Before interviewing for a Police Chief role, I made sure to study the city's crime statistics and attended city council meetings to understand the local political climate.

For corporate interviews, research should include the company's financial performance, market position, and culture. Knowing how the company fits into its industry and having insight into its competitors shows that you've done your homework. Asking insightful questions based on your research helps you stand out as someone who is truly invested in the organization's future.

8. Understanding the Role

Whether you're applying for a law enforcement position or a corporate leadership role, it's important to fully understand the expectations of the job. For external candidates, explaining how you'll transition into the new role and overcome the outsider challenge is key. For internal candidates, emphasizing your existing knowledge of the organization and how it positions you to succeed is equally important.

In business, understanding the organization's strategic goals and aligning your leadership approach with these objectives demonstrates you've thought deeply about how to contribute to the company's success. Discussing how your skills can help achieve the organization's goals positions you as a forward-thinking candidate.

9. Study the Budget and Social Media

Knowing the organization's budget and social media presence can give you an edge. In law enforcement, understanding the department's financial constraints allows you to speak intelligently about resource management and offer solutions. Reviewing the department's public image on social media also gives insight into how the community views the police.

In corporate settings, studying the budget helps you gauge the financial health of the company. If you're interviewing for a management role, discussing budget strategies, cost control, and financial projections will demonstrate your ability to manage resources wisely. Additionally, understanding the company's social media presence can offer insights into its brand image and customer perception.

10. Have Your Answers Ready

Prepare for common interview questions, but don't memorize them. Whether you're asked how you handle disciplinary matters in law enforcement or how you approach crisis management in a corporate setting, being ready with thoughtful, authentic responses is critical. Use examples from your career to illustrate your decision-making and leadership skills.

For law enforcement, you might discuss how you managed a public relations crisis after an officer-involved shooting, focusing on transparency and community engagement. In the corporate world, you could provide an example of how you led a team through a product recall or financial downturn, highlighting the importance of clear communication and decisive action.

11. Personalize Yourself

Sharing aspects of your personal life helps the interviewers see you as a well-rounded individual. In law enforcement, I often talk about my upbringing in a military family, which taught me how to adapt to new environments quickly and build relationships—qualities that have been critical in my leadership roles.

In corporate interviews, sharing personal experiences, such as how your family or hobbies have shaped your leadership style, can create a connection with the interviewers. For example, if you're passionate about community service, discussing how that influences your leadership approach demonstrates that you are not only committed to professional success but also to making a broader positive impact.

12. Show How Much You Care

Passion and enthusiasm are crucial in any interview. Whether you're applying for a law enforcement or corporate leadership role, showing that you genuinely care about the organization and its mission will set you apart. Let your commitment to making a positive impact shine through in your responses.

When I interviewed for leadership roles in law enforcement, I always expressed my dedication to community safety and my desire to build strong relationships between the police department and the community. In the corporate world, demonstrating your passion for the company's vision, whether it's driving innovation or improving customer satisfaction, shows that you're not just looking for a job but are excited about making a meaningful contribution.

Tying it All Together

Interviews are your chance to showcase not only your qualifications but your leadership style, adaptability, and ability to create positive change. Whether you're interviewing for a leadership role in law enforcement or the private sector, the strategies outlined in this section will help you present yourself as a well-rounded, capable leader. Tailor your approach to fit the organization, demonstrate your value, and let your passion for leadership drive you to success.

BONUS SECTION : PERFECTING THE INTERVIEW TO LAND THE POSITION YOU DESIRE

Reflect and Apply: The interview process is your opportunity to demonstrate your leadership potential and communicate how your experience, values, and vision align with the organization's goals. Reflect on the strategies outlined in this section—such as balancing confidence with humility, reframing challenges into opportunities for growth, and asking insightful questions. Assess how well you are preparing for interviews and where you can improve. Use the **Appendix - Leadership Workbook and Action Plans** to craft your interview techniques, refine your personal story, and ensure that you are presenting yourself as the best candidate for your next leadership role.

BONUS SECTION: THE ESSENTIAL TRAITS OF A SUCCESSFUL LEADER

Success in leadership is not just about the actions you take or the decisions you make—it's about the traits you cultivate within yourself. These traits serve as the foundation for everything you do, guiding your choices and shaping your impact on others. As you continue to develop your leadership skills, consider these essential traits that will help you not only succeed but thrive in your leadership journey.

Setting Clear Goals

Goals are the targets that give your leadership direction and purpose. Without goals, leadership can become aimless, reactive, and unfocused. To be successful, you need to set clear, achievable goals that align with your vision and values. These goals give you something to aim for, and they help you measure progress along the way. Whether it's improving team performance, enhancing community relations, or achieving a specific outcome, having clear goals keeps you focused and motivated.

Think of it like going to the shooting range without having a target to shoot at, yet still claiming you're a great shot. Without a target, there's no way to measure your success or identify areas where you need to improve. In life and leadership, goals act as the target—giving you a clear focus to aim for and helping you determine whether you're hitting the mark. They allow you to assess if you're on track or need to make adjustments along the way to hit the bullseye.

In addition to professional goals, it's essential to have a plan for personal growth. As a leader, you should aim to grow not just in your role but also as an individual. For example, focus on developing your personality, enhancing how you influence and inspire others, and improving your communication skills. Personal development must be a part of any set of goals in order to find overall success and balance. Leaders who focus on their personal growth tend to foster better relationships, exhibit more emotional intelligence, and are more adaptable to change. Striving for balance between personal and professional development is key to becoming a well-rounded, impactful leader.

Consistency

Consistency is important in life in general. Developing habits can be positive or negative, depending upon the habit. Spending just 15 minutes a day on something for self-improvement adds up to over 90 hours a year devoted to that task. In leadership, consistency is key to building trust and credibility. As a leader, your team looks to you for stability and reliability. Being consistent in your actions, decisions, and communication ensures that others know what to expect from you. It helps create a stable environment where your team can operate effectively and confidently. Consistency also means not giving up when faced with setbacks. If you remain consistent in pursuing your goals, success will eventually follow.

Happiness

A positive and happy leader inspires those around them. While leadership comes with its challenges, maintaining a sense of happiness and contentment can help you navigate difficult situations with grace. Happiness doesn't mean ignoring challenges—it means finding joy in the journey and bringing a positive attitude to your leadership role. A happy leader creates a positive work environment, which in turn fosters productivity and morale among the team.

Finding Your Purpose

Understanding your purpose is crucial to effective leadership. It's the deeper "why" behind what you do that gives meaning to your work and drives your commitment. Your purpose serves as an inner compass, guiding your decisions and actions in alignment with your core values and passions. Leading with purpose not only motivates you but also inspires those around you to find their own sense of purpose and align their efforts with a shared vision. When you take the time to reflect on what truly matters to you, you create a legacy that transcends individual accomplishments and leads to greater fulfillment and long-term success.

Faith and Spirituality

For many leaders, faith and spirituality are sources of strength, guidance, and comfort. As a Christian, my faith has been a cornerstone in helping me navigate challenges that I may not fully understand. I trust that God has a plan, and I believe that He never gives me more than I can handle. My faith humbles me, reminding me that something greater than myself is in control. This perspective allows me to see perceived obstacles as stepping stones to something greater. Whether in times of difficulty or success, faith can provide the resilience to push forward and the humility to recognize that we are part of a larger purpose.

Love and Compassion

Leadership grounded in love and compassion is leadership that truly cares. When you lead with love, you prioritize the well-being of your team, your community, and the people you serve. Compassionate leadership fosters empathy, understanding, and kindness—qualities that build strong relationships and create a supportive environment. Showing genuine care for others strengthens your influence and creates a lasting positive impact.

Health and Well-being

Your health is the foundation of your ability to lead effectively. Physical, mental, emotional, and spiritual well-being are all critical to maintaining the energy, focus, and resilience required for leadership. Prioritize self-care, exercise, and healthy habits to ensure you're at your best. For me, daily physical fitness is not just about staying in shape—it's a routine that keeps me grounded and focused. Taking care of yourself is necessary for sustaining your ability to lead and support others.

Positivity and Optimism

Positivity and optimism are powerful leadership traits that can transform challenges into opportunities. Maintaining a positive outlook means focusing on the "glass half full" rather than the "glass half empty." You cannot always control what happens to you, but you can control how you respond to it. People see the strength of a leader most clearly in times of adversity. Being optimistic and positive in those moments not only keeps you grounded but also sets the tone for your team. Always find the good in every situation, but be mindful not to take unnecessary risks. Positivity encourages a proactive mindset, and optimism helps create a culture where success feels achievable, even in the face of challenges.

Caring for Others

To lead effectively, you must genuinely care about the people you lead. This means listening to their needs, supporting their growth, and being there for them in times of difficulty. Caring leadership builds trust, loyalty, and a sense of belonging within your team. It's not enough to lead with authority; you must lead with empathy and compassion. When your team knows that you care, they are more likely to go above and beyond in their efforts, contributing to a stronger and more cohesive organization.

Conclusion: The Path to Leadership Success

Success in leadership is not a destination but a continuous journey of growth and self-discovery. The traits discussed in this bonus section—goal setting, consistency, happiness, purpose, faith, love, health, positivity, and caring—are not just qualities to aspire to; they are essential components of a fulfilling and impactful leadership journey.

As you move forward, remember that true leadership is about more than achieving goals or wielding influence. It's about making a positive difference in the lives of others, staying true to your values, and continually striving to be the best version of yourself. Embrace these traits, cultivate them within yourself, and use them to guide your actions as a leader. In doing so, you'll not only achieve success but also create a lasting legacy of leadership that others will look up to and be inspired by.

BONUS SECTION : THE ESSENTIAL TRAITS OF A SUCCESSFUL LEADER

Reflect and Apply: The traits of a successful leader are the foundation of long-term personal and professional growth. Reflect on the essential traits covered in this section—such as setting clear goals, maintaining positivity, and caring for others—and assess how well you embody these qualities. Turn to the **Appendix - Leadership Workbook and Action Plans** to document your personal leadership traits, identify areas for growth, and create a plan to cultivate these characteristics in your day-to-day leadership journey.

150 LEADERSHIP QUESTIONS AND ANSWERS

This section is designed to help you quickly review and polish your leadership skills. Whether you're preparing for a leadership role, managing a team, or seeking to improve your effectiveness, these questions and answers will serve as a handy reference guide.

1. What is the most important trait of a leader?
- Integrity. A leader must be trustworthy and consistent in their actions.

2. How can a leader build trust within a team?
- By being transparent, consistent, and reliable in their actions and communication.

3. What role does communication play in leadership?
- Communication is crucial; it ensures that everyone is on the same page and fosters transparency.

4. How can a leader effectively manage a crisis?
- Stay calm, assess the situation quickly, communicate clearly, and make decisive actions.

5. What is the significance of setting goals?
- Goals provide direction, focus, and a clear target for the team to work towards.

6. How should a leader handle conflict within a team?
- Address it directly and fairly, listen to all parties, and seek a resolution that benefits the team.

7. What is the role of empathy in leadership?
- Empathy helps a leader understand and relate to their team, fostering a supportive environment.

8. **How can a leader inspire their team?**
   - By leading by example, showing passion for the work, and recognizing the contributions of team members.
9. **What is the importance of adaptability in leadership?**
   - Adaptability allows a leader to navigate changes and challenges effectively, keeping the team on track.
10. **How does a leader maintain consistency?**
    - By setting clear expectations, following through on commitments, and aligning actions with values.
11. **What is the best way to give constructive feedback?**
    - Be specific, focus on behavior (not the person), and offer actionable suggestions for improvement.
12. **How can a leader foster innovation within a team?**
    - Encourage creativity, support risk-taking, and create a safe space for sharing new ideas.
13. **What is the role of accountability in leadership?**
    - Accountability ensures that everyone, including the leader, takes responsibility for their actions and outcomes.
14. **How can a leader improve team collaboration?**
    - Facilitate open communication, define clear roles, and encourage mutual respect among team members.
15. **Why is self-awareness important for a leader?**
    - Self-awareness helps leaders understand their strengths, weaknesses, and impact on others, enabling personal growth and better decision-making.
16. **How should a leader approach decision-making?**
    - Gather all relevant information, consider the implications, consult with stakeholders, and make a timely decision.
17. **What is the importance of delegation in leadership?**
    - Delegation empowers team members, builds trust, and allows the leader to focus on higher-level tasks.
18. **How can a leader build resilience in their team?**
    - Encourage a positive mindset, provide support during setbacks, and model perseverance.

19. What is the significance of purpose in leadership?
- Purpose gives meaning to the work, motivates the team, and aligns efforts towards a common goal.

20. How can a leader ensure ethical behavior within a team?
- Set a strong example, establish clear ethical guidelines, and hold everyone accountable to those standards.

21. Why is listening an important leadership skill?
- Active listening builds trust, shows respect, and helps a leader understand the needs and concerns of their team.

22. How can a leader balance short-term demands with long-term goals?
- Prioritize tasks, delegate effectively, and keep the long-term vision in mind when making decisions.

23. What is the role of optimism in leadership?
- Optimism helps maintain morale, motivates the team, and encourages perseverance in the face of challenges.

24. How does a leader build credibility?
- By consistently delivering on promises, being honest, and demonstrating expertise in their field.

25. What is the importance of continuous learning for a leader?
- Continuous learning keeps a leader adaptable, informed, and capable of leading effectively in a changing environment.

26. How can a leader manage stress?
- Practice self-care, delegate tasks, maintain a work-life balance, and seek support when needed.

27. What is the impact of a leader's attitude on the team?
- A leader's attitude sets the tone for the team's culture, influencing morale, productivity, and overall success.

28. How should a leader handle failure?
- Accept responsibility, learn from the experience, and use it as an opportunity for growth and improvement.

29. What is the role of vision in leadership?
- Vision provides a clear direction for the future, guiding the team's efforts and inspiring them to achieve great things.

30. **How can a leader encourage diversity and inclusion?**
    - Foster an open and respectful environment, actively seek diverse perspectives, and implement inclusive policies.
31. **What is the significance of gratitude in leadership?**
    - Expressing gratitude strengthens relationships, boosts morale, and creates a positive work environment.
32. **How can a leader improve their decision-making skills?**
    - Practice critical thinking, seek diverse input, and reflect on past decisions to learn and improve.
33. **Why is humility important in leadership?**
    - Humility allows leaders to acknowledge their limitations, accept feedback, and value the contributions of others.
34. **How does a leader build a strong organizational culture?**
    - Define clear values, model desired behaviors, and consistently reinforce the culture through actions and communication.
35. **What is the role of transparency in leadership?**
    - Transparency builds trust, ensures accountability, and keeps everyone informed and aligned with organizational goals.
36. **How can a leader manage change effectively?**
    - Communicate the reasons for change, involve the team in the process, and provide support throughout the transition.
37. **What is the importance of empathy in leadership?**
    - Empathy helps leaders connect with their team, understand their needs, and create a supportive work environment.
38. **How can a leader foster a growth mindset?**
    - Encourage learning, praise effort and improvement, and view challenges as opportunities for development.
39. **What is the role of discipline in leadership?**
    - Discipline ensures that goals are met, standards are maintained, and the leader remains focused and consistent.
40. **How does a leader inspire confidence?**
    - By demonstrating competence, making informed decisions, and consistently delivering results.

41. **What is the significance of ethical leadership?**
    - Ethical leadership builds trust, upholds organizational values, and ensures that decisions are made with integrity.
42. **How can a leader handle criticism?**
    - Listen to the feedback, assess its validity, and use it as an opportunity to improve.
43. **What is the impact of positivity on a team?**
    - Positivity boosts morale, enhances creativity, and helps the team persevere through challenges.
44. **How does a leader cultivate loyalty?**
    - By showing respect, recognizing contributions, and consistently supporting the team.
45. **What is the importance of strategic thinking in leadership?**
    - Strategic thinking allows leaders to plan for the future, anticipate challenges, and make informed decisions that align with long-term goals.
46. **How can a leader manage difficult conversations?**
    - Prepare in advance, stay calm, focus on the issue, and aim for a constructive resolution.
47. **What is the role of innovation in leadership?**
    - Innovation drives growth, keeps the organization competitive, and encourages continuous improvement.
48. **How can a leader balance authority and approachability?**
    - Be firm and fair in decision-making while remaining open and accessible to your team.
49. **What is the significance of accountability in leadership?**
    - Accountability ensures that leaders and team members are responsible for their actions and outcomes, fostering a culture of trust and reliability.
50. **How does a leader develop others?**
    - Provide opportunities for growth, offer mentorship, and encourage team members to take on new challenges.

51. **What is the role of curiosity in leadership?**
    - Curiosity drives innovation, encourages continuous learning, and helps leaders stay informed and adaptable.
52. **How can a leader improve time management?**
    - Prioritize tasks, delegate when possible, and set clear deadlines to stay on track.
53. **What is the impact of a leader's mindset on their team?**
    - A leader's mindset influences the team's approach to challenges, their resilience, and their overall performance.
54. **How does a leader foster a collaborative environment?**
    - Encourage open communication, value diverse perspectives, and create opportunities for teamwork.
55. **What is the importance of setting clear expectations?**
    - Clear expectations provide direction, reduce confusion, and ensure that everyone is working towards the same goals.
56. **How can a leader build resilience in themselves?**
    - Practice self-care, stay focused on long-term goals, and maintain a positive outlook even in difficult times.
57. **What is the role of delegation in leadership?**
    - Delegation allows leaders to focus on strategic tasks while empowering team members to take ownership I'll continue from where I left off:
57. **What is the role of delegation in leadership?**
    - Delegation allows leaders to focus on strategic tasks while empowering team members to take ownership of specific responsibilities.
58. **How can a leader cultivate a sense of ownership in their team?**
    - By involving team members in decision-making processes and holding them accountable for their outcomes.
59. **What is the importance of patience in leadership?**
    - Patience allows leaders to give their team time to grow, make decisions thoughtfully, and navigate challenges calmly.

60. How does a leader maintain motivation within the team?
- Through recognition, providing clear goals, offering opportunities for growth, and maintaining a positive work environment.

61. What is the significance of humility in leadership?
- Humility enables leaders to acknowledge their limitations, learn from others, and appreciate their team's contributions.

62. How should a leader approach risk management?
- Assess potential risks, plan for contingencies, and take calculated risks when necessary to achieve goals.

63. What is the role of ethics in decision-making?
- Ethics guide leaders to make decisions that align with moral values and the greater good, ensuring long-term trust and respect.

64. How can a leader foster a learning culture?
- Encourage continuous development, support experimentation, and create an environment where mistakes are seen as opportunities for learning.

65. What is the importance of having a vision in leadership?
- A vision provides a clear direction and inspiration for the team, guiding their efforts and aligning their actions with long-term goals.

66. How does a leader handle uncertainty?
- By staying informed, remaining flexible, and communicating openly with the team to navigate through uncertain times.

67. What is the role of respect in leadership?
- Respect fosters a positive work environment, strengthens relationships, and ensures that everyone feels valued and heard.

68. How can a leader ensure continuous improvement?
- Regularly evaluate processes, encourage feedback, and stay open to change to improve efficiency and effectiveness.

69. **What is the significance of courage in leadership?**
    - Courage allows leaders to take bold actions, make difficult decisions, and stand by their values even in the face of opposition.
70. **How does a leader build and maintain credibility?**
    - Through consistent actions, transparency, honesty, and demonstrating expertise in their field.
71. **What is the role of emotional intelligence in leadership?**
    - Emotional intelligence enables leaders to understand and manage their own emotions and the emotions of others, leading to better relationships and decision-making.
72. **How can a leader manage team dynamics effectively?**
    - By understanding each team member's strengths and weaknesses, fostering collaboration, and addressing conflicts constructively.
73. **What is the importance of self-reflection in leadership?**
    - Self-reflection helps leaders understand their own actions, learn from past experiences, and continuously improve.
74. **How should a leader handle success?**
    - Celebrate achievements with the team, recognize contributions, and stay focused on future goals without becoming complacent.
75. **What is the impact of mentorship in leadership?**
    - Mentorship provides guidance, support, and development opportunities for both the mentor and mentee, fostering growth and knowledge sharing.
76. **How can a leader create a culture of accountability?**
    - Set clear expectations, provide regular feedback, and hold everyone responsible for their actions and outcomes.
77. **What is the role of strategic thinking in leadership?**
    - Strategic thinking enables leaders to plan for the future, anticipate challenges, and make decisions that align with long-term goals.

78. How does a leader build a strong organizational culture?
- By defining and modeling core values, consistently reinforcing desired behaviors, and creating an environment that supports the culture.

79. What is the significance of adaptability in leadership?
- Adaptability allows leaders to respond effectively to change, pivot when necessary, and lead their team through uncertainty.

80. How can a leader foster innovation within their team?
- Encourage creative thinking, support experimentation, and provide the resources and environment necessary for innovation to thrive.

81. What is the role of perseverance in leadership?
- Perseverance helps leaders stay focused on their goals, overcome obstacles, and lead their team through challenging times.

82. How does a leader maintain focus on long-term goals?
- By setting clear priorities, avoiding distractions, and regularly reviewing progress toward long-term objectives.

83. What is the importance of recognizing and rewarding success?
- Recognition and rewards boost morale, motivate the team, and reinforce desired behaviors and outcomes.

84. How can a leader maintain a positive work-life balance?
- By setting boundaries, prioritizing self-care, and managing time effectively to ensure both professional and personal well-being.

85. What is the role of vision in inspiring a team?
- A compelling vision motivates the team, provides a sense of purpose, and aligns their efforts with a shared goal.

86. How does a leader build resilience in their team?
- By fostering a supportive environment, encouraging a positive mindset, and helping the team navigate setbacks and challenges.

87. What is the significance of diversity in leadership?
- Diversity brings different perspectives, enhances creativity, and leads to more inclusive and effective decision-making.

88. How can a leader effectively manage change?
- By communicating the reasons for change, involving the team in the process, and providing the support needed to adapt.

89. What is the importance of feedback in leadership?
- Feedback helps leaders and team members understand strengths and areas for improvement, driving continuous growth and development.

90. How can a leader maintain motivation and enthusiasm?
- By staying passionate about their work, setting inspiring goals, and recognizing the achievements of the team.

91. What is the role of trust in leadership?
- Trust is the foundation of effective leadership, enabling open communication, collaboration, and a positive team environment.

92. How can a leader develop a strong personal brand?
- By consistently demonstrating their values, expertise, and leadership style in all interactions and communications.

93. What is the significance of empathy in leadership?
- Empathy allows leaders to connect with their team, understand their needs, and create a supportive and inclusive environment.

94. How does a leader foster a culture of continuous learning?
- Encourage curiosity, provide opportunities for development, and model a commitment to learning and growth.

95. What is the impact of a leader's attitude on their team?
- A leader's attitude influences the team's morale, productivity, and overall success, setting the tone for the work environment.

96. How can a leader handle difficult conversation?
- By preparing in advance, staying calm, focusing on the issue at hand, and seeking a constructive resolution.

97. What is the role of confidence in leadership?
- Confidence helps leaders make decisions, inspire their team, and navigate challenges with assurance and poise.

98. How can a leader build a high-performing team?
- By selecting the right people, providing clear goals, fostering collaboration, and supporting ongoing development.

99. What is the importance of purpose in leadership?
- Purpose gives meaning to the work, aligns the team's efforts with a shared goal, and motivates everyone to contribute their best.

100. How does a leader leave a lasting legacy?
- By consistently leading with integrity, making a positive impact on others, and creating a culture that reflects their values long after they're gone.

101. How can a leader foster trust in a remote work environment?
- Consistent communication, transparency, and delivering on commitments build trust even when working remotely.

102. What is the role of body language in leadership?
- Positive body language can reinforce verbal communication, convey confidence, and build rapport.

103. How should a leader handle workplace gossip?
- Address it directly by fostering a culture of open communication and discouraging negative talk.

104. How can a leader ensure ethical behavior in their team?
- Model ethical behavior, establish clear guidelines, and hold everyone accountable.

105. What is the impact of a leader's tone of voice?
- A leader's tone can influence the mood, motivation, and receptivity of the team.

106. How can a leader cultivate patience in their leadership style?
- Practice active listening, avoid rushing decisions, and give team members time to grow.

107. What is the significance of mentorship in leadership development?
- Mentorship provides guidance, shares experience, and helps develop future leaders.

108. How can a leader build cross-functional teams?
- Encourage collaboration across departments, define clear roles, and focus on shared goals.

109. What is the importance of self-reflection in leadership?
- Self-reflection helps leaders learn from experiences, improve decision-making, and enhance their leadership style.

110. How can a leader effectively manage organizational change?
- Communicate the reasons for change, involve the team in the process, and provide support during the transition.

111. What is the role of vulnerability in leadership?
- Showing vulnerability builds trust, fosters connection, and encourages openness within the team.

112. How can a leader improve team decision-making?
- Encourage diverse perspectives, facilitate discussions, and guide the team toward a consensus.

113. What is the impact of a leader's consistency?
- Consistency builds trust, sets expectations, and creates a stable environment for the team.

114. How can a leader manage a crisis effectively?
- Stay calm, gather accurate information, communicate clearly, and act decisively.

115. What is the role of gratitude in leadership?
- Expressing gratitude strengthens relationships, boosts morale, and encourages a positive work culture.

116. How can a leader balance empathy and authority?
- Show understanding while maintaining clear expectations and boundaries.

117. What is the importance of adaptability in a rapidly changing environment?
- Adaptability allows leaders to respond effectively to new challenges and opportunities.

118. How can a leader handle a toxic work environment?
- Identify the root causes, address issues directly, and work to rebuild a positive culture.

119. What is the role of perseverance in leadership?
- Perseverance helps leaders overcome obstacles, maintain focus, and inspire their teams to keep pushing forward.

120. How can a leader support employee well-being?
- Encourage work-life balance, provide resources for mental health, and promote a healthy work environment.

121. What is the impact of a leader's punctuality?
- Being punctual shows respect for others' time, sets a positive example, and reinforces discipline.

122. How can a leader foster a culture of continuous improvement?
- Encourage feedback, support professional development, and celebrate incremental progress.

123. What is the importance of setting boundaries as a leader?
- Boundaries help maintain a healthy work-life balance and prevent burnout.

124. How can a leader build resilience in themselves?
- Practice stress management, maintain a positive outlook, and learn from setbacks.

125. What is the role of a leader in conflict resolution?
- Facilitate open dialogue, listen to all parties, and guide the team toward a fair resolution.

126. How can a leader inspire innovation?
- Create a safe environment for experimentation, recognize creative efforts, and encourage new ideas.

127. What is the significance of active problem-solving in leadership?
- Active problem-solving demonstrates leadership competence and helps resolve issues quickly and effectively.

128. How can a leader maintain focus during high-pressure situations?
- Prioritize tasks, delegate when necessary, and remain calm under pressure.

129. What is the importance of a leader's vision?
- A clear vision provides direction, motivates the team, and aligns efforts with long-term goals.

130. How can a leader handle difficult conversations?
- Prepare in advance, approach the conversation with empathy, and focus on solutions.

131. What is the impact of recognition on team dynamics?
- Recognition strengthens relationships, boosts morale, and encourages continued excellence.

132. How can a leader manage competing priorities?
- Assess the impact of each task, prioritize based on importance and urgency, and delegate when appropriate.

133. What is the role of flexibility in leadership?
- Flexibility allows leaders to adapt to changing circumstances and meet the diverse needs of their team.

134. How can a leader foster accountability in the team?
- Set clear expectations, provide regular feedback, and hold everyone responsible for their actions.

135. What is the importance of clear communication in leadership?
- Clear communication ensures that everyone understands their roles, responsibilities, and the overall mission.

136. How can a leader handle resistance to change?
- Address concerns, involve the team in the process, and demonstrate the benefits of the change.

137. What is the role of a leader in building team morale?
- Recognize achievements, provide support, and create a positive work environment.

138. How can a leader encourage ownership within the team?
- Delegate responsibilities, provide autonomy, and recognize contributions.

139. What is the importance of leading by example?
- Leading by example sets the standard for behavior and performance, inspiring the team to follow suit.

140. How can a leader ensure they are approachable?
- Maintain open communication, be available for discussions, and listen without judgment.

141. What is the role of self-discipline in leadership?
- Self-discipline ensures that leaders stay focused, meet their commitments, and model desired behaviors.

142. How can a leader manage expectations from stakeholders?
- Communicate clearly, set realistic goals, and provide regular updates on progress.

143. What is the impact of a leader's confidence on their team?
- A leader's confidence can inspire trust, motivate the team, and encourage bold actions.

144. How can a leader address performance issues?
- Provide specific feedback, set clear improvement goals, and offer support and resources.

145. What is the importance of continuous feedback in leadership?
- Continuous feedback helps employees grow, improve performance, and stay aligned with organizational goals.

146. How can a leader foster a culture of accountability?
- Set clear expectations, monitor progress, and ensure that everyone is held accountable for their actions.

147. What is the role of optimism in leading a team?
- Optimism helps maintain morale, encourages resilience, and creates a positive work environment.

148. How can a leader navigate complex decisions?
- Gather all relevant information, weigh the pros and cons, and consult with key stakeholders.

149. What is the significance of cultural awareness in leadership?
- Cultural awareness helps leaders understand and respect diverse perspectives, fostering an inclusive environment.

150. How can a leader build strong relationships with their team?
- Show genuine interest in team members, provide support, and maintain open, honest communication.

APPENDIX- LEADERSHIP WORKBOOK AND ACTION PLANS

Purpose and Intent:

This workbook section is designed as a tool to help you reflect on your leadership journey and apply the principles and lessons from *Leadership Under Fire: Lessons from the Frontlines of Law Enforcement*. Use this guide to document your thoughts, identify areas for growth, and create actionable plans to enhance your leadership skills. Over time, you can revisit this workbook to see how far you've come and how your leadership style has evolved. Remember, the goal of leadership is continual improvement—both for yourself and the people you lead.

CHAPTER 1: LEADING WITH INTEGRITY

Reflection Questions:

1. What does integrity mean to you in your current leadership role, especially when facing resistance or pressure to compromise your values?
2. Recall a time when you had to make a tough ethical decision, even when your supervisor or colleagues disagreed. How did you ensure your decision was rooted in integrity?
3. How do you foster a culture of accountability and transparency within your team, especially when dealing with difficult situations like discipline or terminations?
4. How do you balance standing firm on your principles while maintaining professional relationships with those in authority?

Action Plan:

1. **Set Personal Integrity Goals:** Write down 3-5 integrity goals that guide your leadership decisions and actions.
    a. *Example:* I will ensure that all my decisions are ethical, even when they may be unpopular with leadership or peers.
2. **Assess Current Practices:** Reflect on recent decisions to see if they aligned with your ethical values. Identify areas where improvements can be made.
    a. *Example:* I will re-examine how I handle internal audits and tough decisions, ensuring transparency and accountability at all levels.
3. **Strengthen Accountability:** Develop a system for holding yourself and your team accountable for ethical behavior.
    a. *Example:* I will encourage open dialogue with my team to address potential ethical concerns and ensure transparency in all actions.
4. **Build a Culture of Integrity:** Identify ways to instill integrity in your team's daily operations.
    a. *Example:* I will create a mentorship program to emphasize ethical decision-making and lead by example to show that integrity is the foundation of success.

CHAPTER 2 : DISCOVERING YOUR LEADERSHIP IDENTITY

Reflection Questions:

1. Which leadership style resonates with you the most, and why?
2. Have you blended different leadership styles in the past? How did it benefit your team?
3. How can you adapt your leadership style in different situations?

Action Plan:

1. **Assess Your Leadership Style:**
2. Complete the sentence: "As a leader, I am primarily _____, but I also embrace aspects of _____."
3. **Set Leadership Development Goals:**
4. Choose 2-3 leadership styles that you want to develop further. Write down actionable steps to build those skills.

Example: I will work on being a more strategic leader by dedicating time each week for long-term planning.

CHAPTER 3 : PROACTIVE LEADERSHIP: A PATH TO SUCCESS

Reflection Questions:

1. Reflect on a recent leadership decision: Was it reactive or proactive? How could a proactive approach have changed the outcome?
2. In your current role, how do you actively anticipate challenges, and how do you ensure you're taking steps to prevent potential issues?
3. Consider a time when you were faced with a crisis. How did your level of proactivity (or reactivity) influence the result?
4. How can you develop a more proactive culture within your team, ensuring that problems are addressed before they escalate?

Action Plan:

1. **Evaluate Your Current Proactive Practices:**
    a. **Task:** Identify one or two areas within your team or organization where you often find yourself reacting to problems. What systems or strategies can you implement to move from reactive to proactive leadership?
    b. **Example:** I will hold monthly strategy meetings to identify potential challenges and solutions ahead of time.
2. **Set Proactive Leadership Goals:**
    a. **Task:** Write down 3-5 goals that focus on proactive leadership in your current position.
    b. **Example:** I will create a risk assessment framework for my team to help identify potential issues in upcoming projects.
3. **Implement a Feedback Loop:**
    a. **Task:** Develop a system that encourages your team to provide feedback on potential risks or problems. This can help you address concerns before they become larger issues.

b. **Example:** I will implement quarterly feedback surveys where team members can voice concerns or suggest areas that need attention.
4. **Blend Proactive Leadership Across Sectors:**
   a. **Task:** Consider how proactive leadership could apply differently in a private sector role compared to a public service role. What adjustments would you make to your strategies?
   b. **Example:** In the private sector, I will focus on proactively managing customer satisfaction by identifying trends and complaints early, allowing for swift resolution before they escalate.
5. **Build a Culture of Proactivity:**
   a. **Task:** Encourage proactive thinking within your team by promoting initiatives where members are rewarded for preemptive problem-solving.
   b. **Example:** I will create an incentive program that recognizes employees who successfully identify and resolve potential issues before they impact the organization.

CHAPTER 4 : CRISIS MANAGEMENT

Reflection Questions:

1. How do you currently prepare for crises?
2. What have been the most significant crises you've faced, and how did you handle them?
3. How can you improve your communication and leadership during a crisis?

Action Plan:

1. **Develop a Crisis Action Plan:**
    a. Identify three potential crises that could occur in your organization and outline steps to manage them.
2. **Enhance Your Crisis Communication:**
    a. Develop a template for communicating with your team during a crisis. Practice delivering clear and composed messages.

CHAPTER 5 : BUILDING AND LEADING EFFECTIVE TEAMS

Reflection Questions:

1. What steps do you take to build trust within your team?
2. How do you foster communication and accountability?
3. In what ways can you empower your team more effectively?

Action Plan:

1. **Establish Clear Communication Practices:**
    a. Identify ways to improve communication within your team (e.g., regular check-ins or briefings).
2. **Develop a Team Empowerment Strategy:**
    a. Write down 2-3 ways you can encourage leadership development within your team members.

CHAPTER 6 : COMMUNITY-CENTERED LEADERSHIP

Reflection Questions:

1. How do you engage with your community or stakeholders?
2. What steps can you take to build trust and transparency in your organization?
3. How do you serve the needs of diverse communities within your organization?

Action Plan:

1. **Build a Community Engagement Plan:**
    a. Identify specific actions you can take to engage directly with your community or client base.
2. **Assess Inclusivity Efforts:**
    a. List ways to promote inclusivity and cultural awareness in your leadership style.

CHAPTER 7 : THE ABILITY TO MAKE DECISIONS

Reflection Questions:

1. What fears, if any, have held you back from making decisive decisions?
2. How do you own your mistakes as a leader?
3. How do your decisions shape the culture of your organization?

Action Plan:

1. **Strengthen Decisiveness:**
    a. Identify three situations where you will practice more decisive leadership.
2. **Own Your Leadership Mistakes:**
    a. Reflect on a past mistake, and outline steps to prevent it from happening again. Communicate this growth with your team.

CHAPTER 8 : ACCOUNTABILITY AND DISCIPLINE IN LEADERSHIP

Reflection Questions:

1. How do you approach progressive discipline in your leadership role, and how do you ensure it is applied fairly and consistently?
2. Have you encountered a situation where an employee refused to take accountability? How did you handle it, and what did you learn?
3. What systems do you have in place to hold employees accountable while maintaining team morale?
4. How do you balance addressing misconduct with preserving the dignity of the individual involved?

Action Plan:

1. **Create a Transparent Progressive Discipline Policy:** Document the steps for progressive discipline, ensuring clarity and fairness in all instances.
2. **Build a Culture of Accountability:** Incorporate clear expectations for responsibility and accountability at every level of the organization.
3. **Plan for Difficult Conversations:** Prepare for tough discussions by developing strategies to address accountability issues with empathy and respect.
4. **Preserve Dignity in Disciplinary Actions:** Ensure that all discipline is conducted discreetly and professionally, preserving the individual's dignity.

CHAPTER 9 : TERMINATION AND LAYOFFS WITH COMPASSION

Reflection Questions:

1. What steps do you take to ensure that terminations are justified, ethical, and handled with compassion?
2. How do you maintain team morale after a termination or layoff?
3. Have you ever had to lay off employees due to financial reasons? How did you support them through the process?
4. How do you communicate difficult decisions, such as terminations or layoffs, with transparency and empathy?

Action Plan:

1. **Develop a Humane Termination Process:** Create clear procedures for handling terminations, ensuring that decisions are justified and communicated with respect.
2. **Provide Support During Layoffs:** Offer career transition resources, personal references, or counseling services for employees affected by layoffs.
3. **Foster Open Communication:** Ensure transparent communication with remaining employees to maintain trust and address concerns following terminations or layoffs.
4. **Focus on Team Morale Post-Termination:** Plan team meetings and support systems to restore morale and trust after personnel changes.

CHAPTER 10 : WHY PEOPLE DON'T QUIT JOBS, THEY QUIT LEADERS

Reflection Questions:

1. How does your leadership style impact employee retention?
2. What steps can you take to improve your team's job satisfaction?
3. How can you create a culture that retains top talent?

Action Plan:

1. **Conduct a Retention Review:**
    a. Assess retention rates within your organization and identify potential areas of improvement.
2. **Create a Retention Strategy:**
    a. Write down specific actions you will take to create a culture that encourages long-term retention.

CHAPTER 11 : THE ART OF DELEGATION AND EMPOWERMENT

Reflection Questions:

1. How comfortable are you with delegating tasks?
2. Do you empower your team members to grow and take initiative?
3. How can you improve the delegation process?

Action Plan:

1. **Delegate More Effectively:**
    a. Identify two tasks you will delegate in the coming week and outline the expected outcomes.
2. **Create a Growth Plan for Team Members:**
    a. Write down strategies for empowering each team member through delegation and leadership development.

CHAPTER 12 : ADAPTING TO CULTURAL CHALLENGES

Reflection Questions:

1. How do you adapt your leadership style when working with a diverse team or community?
2. What cultural challenges have you faced in your leadership role, and how did you overcome them?
3. How can you recruit and empower a more diverse workforce in your organization?

Action Plan:

1. **Develop a Cultural Adaptation Strategy:**
   a. List 2-3 ways you can adjust your leadership to be more culturally aware and inclusive.
2. **Enhance Diversity in Your Team:**
   a. Write down specific actions you will take to recruit and support a diverse workforce.

CHAPTER 13 : LEADERSHIP AND TECHNOLOGY

Reflection Questions:

1. How do you integrate technology into your leadership approach?
2. What role does data-driven decision-making play in your organization?
3. How do you balance the use of technology with maintaining the human element of leadership?

Action Plan:

1. **Leverage Technology for Better Decision-Making:**
    a. Identify three ways you can use technology to improve resource allocation or decision-making in your team.
2. **Enhance Human Interaction:**
    a. Write down 2-3 actions to ensure that technology doesn't replace personal connection and empathy in your leadership style.

CHAPTER 14 : ETHICS AND LEADERSHIP

Reflection Questions:

1. What ethical challenges have you faced in your leadership role?
2. How do you maintain integrity in the face of political or organizational pressure?
3. How do you encourage ethical behavior within your team or organization?

Action Plan:

1. **Strengthen Ethical Practices:**
    a. Outline steps you will take to reinforce ethical behavior and decision-making within your team.
2. **Develop an Ethics Accountability Plan:**
    a. Write down specific actions you will take to ensure that ethical standards are consistently upheld, even in difficult situations.

CHAPTER 15 : NAVIGATING ORGANIZATIONAL POLITICS

Reflection Questions:

1. How do you manage political dynamics within your organization without compromising your integrity?
2. What strategies have helped you maintain neutrality in politically charged environments?
3. How do you communicate effectively with key stakeholders to navigate complex political situations?

Action Plan:

1. **Master Strategic Communication:**
    a. Write down three strategies you will use to improve communication with stakeholders in politically sensitive situations.
2. **Build Political Resilience:**
    a. Identify one or two political challenges you face and create a plan to navigate them while maintaining your integrity.

CHAPTER 16 : ENCOURAGING POSITIVE CULTURE THROUGH CELEBRATING SUCCESSES

Reflection Questions:

1. How do you currently recognize and celebrate successes within your team?
2. How does celebrating successes impact morale and motivation?
3. How can you create a culture that pushes people beyond their comfort zones while fostering loyalty?

Action Plan:

1. **Enhance Recognition:**
    a. Develop a recognition plan to celebrate team successes in meaningful ways.
2. **Create a Growth Plan for Team Members:**
    a. Write down steps to challenge team members to step out of their comfort zones while still supporting them.

CHAPTER 17 : FACING ADVERSITY IN LEADERSHIP

Reflection Questions:

1. How have you responded to adversity in your leadership journey, and what did those experiences teach you?
2. When have your ethical principles been tested, and how did you stand on integrity during those moments?
3. How has your support system helped you navigate challenging times, and how can you cultivate a stronger network of support in the future?

Action Plan:

1. **Identify Key Moments of Adversity:**
    a. List the significant challenges you've faced as a leader and reflect on how you handled them. Identify areas where your response could have been stronger and what you learned from those experiences.
2. **Strengthen Your Support System:**
    a. Write down steps you can take to build and maintain a solid support system—both professionally and personally—to help you navigate future adversities.
3. **Develop Ethical Leadership Strategies:**
    a. Outline specific ways you will uphold your ethical principles in challenging situations and how you will encourage your team to follow suit.

CHAPTER 18 : THRIVING THROUGH ADVERSITY

Reflection Questions:

1. How have setbacks and public scrutiny shaped your leadership style?
2. What strategies have you used to stay resilient and maintain a positive outlook when facing adversity?
3. How do you ensure you surround yourself with the right people who support your leadership journey?

Action Plan:

1. **Turn Setbacks into Opportunities:**
    a. Identify recent challenges you've faced and outline actionable steps to turn them into opportunities for growth and leadership development.
2. **Cultivate a Positive Mindset:**
    a. Create a personal action plan for maintaining a positive outlook, especially during challenging times. This can include setting small, achievable goals and recognizing incremental progress.
3. **Review Your Inner Circle:**
    a. List the people in your professional and personal life who influence your leadership. Identify those who genuinely support your growth and how you can continue fostering those relationships.

CHAPTER 19 : TRANSITIONING LEADERSHIP ACROSS INDUSTRIES

Reflection Questions:

1. What leadership skills have you developed that are universally applicable across law enforcement, corporate, and other sectors?
2. How can crisis management and decision-making skills be adapted to different industries?
3. What steps can you take to balance leadership styles such as collaboration and decisiveness in new environments?
4. How can you maintain personal integrity and ethical standards when transitioning into a different field of leadership?

Action Plan:

1. **Evaluate Your Transferable Skills:** List the leadership skills you've developed in your career—whether in law enforcement, corporate, or another sector—and identify how they can be applied to different roles across industries.
2. **Build a Cross-Industry Leadership Strategy:** Develop a plan that highlights how you can adapt your leadership style to fit both current and future leadership roles. Focus on skills like team management, strategic planning, and communication.
3. **Create a Continuous Learning Path:** Identify areas where you can grow further in your leadership journey. Set goals for acquiring new skills that can enhance your leadership ability across sectors.

CONCLUSION: THE LEGACY OF LEADERSHIP

Reflection Questions:

1. How do you want to be remembered as a leader?
2. What steps are you taking to ensure your leadership has a lasting impact?
3. How can you further develop your leadership skills to leave a meaningful legacy?

Action Plan:

1. **Build Your Leadership Legacy:**
    a. Outline 2-3 actions you will take to build a legacy based on purpose, ethics, and compassion.
2. **Reflect on Your Growth:**
    a. Review your progress from this workbook and write down specific steps to continue your leadership development in the future.

BONUS SECTION: PERFECTING THE INTERVIEW TO LAND THE POSITION YOU DESIRE

Reflection Questions:

1. How well do you balance confidence and humility during interviews? In what ways can you improve this balance?
2. How do you handle discussing past challenges or negative experiences? Are you effectively turning negatives into positives?
3. Do you research the organization and role thoroughly before an interview? What additional steps can you take to ensure you are fully prepared?
4. How well do you tailor your appearance, communication style, and demeanor to fit the expectations of the role or organization?
5. Are you asking insightful and strategic questions during interviews? What additional questions could you prepare to demonstrate your interest and value?

Action Plan:

1. **Enhance Interview Preparation:** Write down 2-3 steps you will take to improve your research and preparation for your next interview, such as studying the organization's financials, social media, or attending relevant public meetings.
2. **Develop Thoughtful Responses:** Identify 2-3 examples from your career that demonstrate your leadership under pressure or your ability to handle challenges. Practice framing these in a positive light, showing how they shaped your growth.
3. **Craft Engaging Questions:** Prepare 2-3 insightful questions you can ask in future interviews that demonstrate your forward-thinking approach and genuine interest in the organization's goals.

BONUS SECTION: THE ESSENTIAL TRAITS OF A SUCCESSFUL LEADER

Reflection Questions:

1. Which traits of a successful leader do you most identify with, and which need further development?
2. How can you embody these traits in your day-to-day leadership?
3. What changes can you make to align more closely with these essential leadership traits?

Action Plan:

1. **Cultivate Key Leadership Traits:**
    a. Write down 2-3 leadership traits you want to develop and create a plan to embody them more consistently.
2. **Track Your Leadership Evolution:**
    a. Set personal goals for each trait and track your progress over time to ensure continuous growth in your leadership journey.

ACKNOWLEDGMENTS AND TRIBUTE

Writing this book has been a journey I could not have completed alone, and I am deeply grateful to the many people who have supported and inspired me along the way.

To my wife, Louise—your unwavering love, patience, and belief in me have been my anchor through every challenge. To my children, Kaleb, Noah, McKenna, and Hunter, as well as my bonus children, Christina and Nick—and my grandchildren, Finny and Lennon—you are my pride and joy, and you inspire me every day to be a better person and leader. I hope this book makes you proud.

To my parents, Craig and Gretchen, and my siblings, Clint and Heather—thank you for the values you instilled in me. Your guidance has shaped who I am today, providing the foundation for everything I have achieved. Your support and encouragement mean the world to me.

I also want to express my immense gratitude to my law enforcement colleagues, both in the United States and across the 30-plus nations with whom I've had the privilege to serve over the years. Your dedication, bravery, and commitment to justice have been a constant source of inspiration. Whether working alongside you in the streets of the United States or in challenging environments overseas, I have learned so much from each of you. This book reflects the collective experiences and lessons we've shared.

To my brothers and sisters in blue who have paid the ultimate sacrifice while fighting to make this world a better place—you are not forgotten. Your courage, dedication, and unwavering commitment to justice inspire us all to continue the work you began. This book is a tribute to your memory and to the enduring legacy you leave behind.

To the communities I have served—thank you for trusting me and allowing me to be part of your lives. Your resilience and spirit have shown me the true meaning of leadership.

Finally, I want to acknowledge everyone who contributed to the creation of this book—editors, advisors, and friends. Your insights and feedback have been invaluable in shaping this work.

Above all, I want to give my deepest and most important thank you to God for allowing me to survive so many challenges. Each trial has molded me into the leader I am today. Without His guidance and grace, I would not be where I am. I look forward to continuing to teach the next generation of leaders while seeking purpose in whichever direction You send me next. My faith has carried me through every adversity, and I trust in God's plan as I continue to grow and serve.

Thank you all for being part of my journey. This book is as much yours as it is mine.

ABOUT THE AUTHOR

Keith Grounsell is a highly respected law enforcement professional with over 26 years of leadership experience across city, county, state, federal, and international levels. He has specialized in crime prevention, community engagement, and special operations targeting drug traffickers, gangs, and terrorists, while also leading efforts to fight corruption. Keith has held several esteemed leadership roles, including serving as a two-time Chief of Police, Lead Investigator for the largest prosecutor's office in South Carolina, and U.S. Contingent Commander for both the United Nations and the U.S. Department of State. His leadership led to transformative changes, such as a remarkable 287% increase in drug-related investigations and guiding one department to become the #1 safest city in the state in under two years.

Keith's career has also taken him to some of the world's most challenging environments. He advised and led specialized police forces in Afghanistan, Haiti, Liberia, Jordan, India, and Nigeria, tackling issues such as corruption, terrorism, and instability. His steadfast commitment to integrity was exemplified when his leadership as Chief of Police led to the indictment and conviction of a corrupt mayor and police officers, demonstrating his resolve to fight corruption at the highest levels, despite the personal and professional risks involved.

As the author of the acclaimed book series *A Narc's Tale*, Keith shares his deep undercover experiences as an undercover city police officer, county vice & narcotics investigator, and special agent with the U.S. Drug Enforcement Administration, which inspired a television series on the A&E network. One powerful story from the series even inspired an award-winning film on human trafficking, shedding light on one of the darkest crimes of our time. Throughout his writing, Keith fully discloses both his successes and mistakes, offering readers raw and candid insights designed to teach and guide the next generation of leaders in law enforcement—and in any organization.

Over the course of his career, Keith has been awarded more than 30 medals and commendations for his leadership in high-pressure, complex environments. His achievements are further backed by academic credentials, including an M.A. in Criminal Justice from American Military University, a B.S. in Sociology with a Criminal Justice emphasis from Lander University, and participation in prestigious leadership programs at the Southern Police Institute (SPI) and the FBI.

Widely recognized for his unwavering dedication to ethical leadership, community service, and justice, Keith's journey is not only inspiring but also serves as a roadmap for those seeking to navigate the complexities of leadership under fire.

OTHER GREAT READS BY THIS SAME AUTHOR

If you've enjoyed this book, I invite you to explore *A NARC'S TALE*, a thrilling four-book series that offers an unprecedented inside look into the dangerous world of undercover narcotics work at the city, county, and federal levels. Across these volumes, I share my experiences working six years deep undercover, from my early days as a city cop to my career as a special agent with the DEA.

All books in *A NARC'S TALE* series are available in paperback, Kindle, and audio formats. You can find and purchase them on Amazon, where readers can dive deeper into these real-life undercover stories filled with danger, intrigue, and the constant fight against drug cartels and criminal organizations.

A NARC'S TALE **Volume 1: "The Beginning"**

In Volume 1, I recount my journey from aspiring officer to full-time undercover city cop. Thrust into the narcotics world without formal training, I learned the ropes through trial and error, managing to take down over 130 drug dealers in my first year. Through raw, unfiltered diary-style storytelling, I take you through the personal and professional challenges I faced in the streets, revealing the life-changing experiences that ignited my passion for drug enforcement.

Cover Image:

A NARC'S TALE Volume 2: "Into the Fire"

Volume 2 transitions into my time working with a large county sheriff's office in the Vice and Narcotics Unit. This book captures my growth as an undercover investigator after receiving proper training, leading to bigger and more dangerous cases. Here, I face tragedy with the drug-related murder of my former partner and expose police corruption while juggling my new role as a husband and father. This volume delves into the personal tolls and risks of undercover work, from multi-kilo drug deals to murder-for-hire operations.

Cover Image:

A NARC'S TALE Volume 3: "Crossing the Line"

In Volume 3, the stakes are higher than ever as I take on large-scale drug operations, including a multi-kilo cocaine deal and a murder-for-hire case. This volume explores the dangers of working undercover, as harassment, threats, and hits on my life become frequent. You'll learn about the advanced undercover tactics I developed and the mental effects of being immersed in this world for so long. As my time in county law enforcement winds down, I prepare to take my undercover skills to the federal level.

Cover Image:

A NARC'S TALE Volume 4: "Going Federal"

Volume 4 marks the pinnacle of my narcotics career as I join the DEA as a Special Agent, working against some of the largest and most dangerous drug cartels in the world. From multi-billion-dollar international drug operations to wiretaps and task forces, this volume provides a detailed account of the sheer scale of federal narcotics investigations. The book also covers my personal frustrations with bureaucracy and the challenges of balancing family life while dealing with unprecedented levels of violence, death, and corruption. In the end, it highlights how my drug enforcement experience was leveraged to achieve success as Chief of Police and in my international work in Afghanistan, Haiti, and Liberia.

Cover Image:

Kaleb's Journey of Kindness: Valuable Lessons to Teach Our Youth

In addition to my work in law enforcement, I am proud to present *Kaleb's Journey of Kindness: Valuable Lessons to Teach Our Youth*, a heartwarming children's book designed to inspire the next generation with lessons of kindness, empathy, and compassion. This touching narrative follows Kaleb, a young boy who embarks on a journey filled with wisdom and life lessons imparted by his grandfather, Craig. As Kaleb navigates the complexities of growing up, he learns the importance of sportsmanship, standing up to bullies, respecting law enforcement, and making responsible choices, including saying 'no' to harmful influences.

Throughout the story, Kaleb also explores gun safety, embraces his faith, and learns to show kindness to animals, with the help of his loyal dog, Capone. Each chapter is filled with engaging illustrations and meaningful lessons, making this book an excellent tool for parents and educators to teach children the values of respect, generosity, and responsibility. *Kaleb's Journey of Kindness* is a reminder that even the smallest acts of kindness can make a big difference in the world, leaving a lasting impact on both the giver and receiver.

This book can be found on Amazon in paperback or Kindle.

Cover Image:

Made in the USA
Columbia, SC
14 January 2025